Cobbett

Past Masters

AQUINAS Anthony Kenny
ARISTOTLE Jonathan Barnes
FRANCIS BACON Anthony Quinton
BAYLE Elisabeth Labrousse
BERKELEY J. O. Urmson
BURKE C. B. Macpherson
CARLYLE A. L. Le Quesne
CLAUSEWITZ Michael Howard
COBBETT Raymond Williams
COLERIDGE Richard Holmes
CONFUCIUS Raymond Dawson
DANTE George Holmes
DARWIN Jonathan Howard
ENGELS Terrell Carver

GALILEO Stillman Drake
HEGEL Peter Singer
HOMER Jasper Griffin
HUME A. J. Ayer
JESUS Humphrey Carpenter
KANT Roger Scruton
MACHIAVELLI Quentin Skinner
MARX Peter Singer
MONTAIGNE Peter Burke
NEWMAN Owen Chadwick
PASCAL Alban Krailsheimer
PLATO R. M. Hare
PROUST Derwent May
TOLSTOY Henry Gifford

Forthcoming

AUGUSTINE Henry Chadwick
BACH Denis Arnold
BERGSON Leszek Kolakowski
THE BUDDHA Michael Carrithers
JOSEPH BUTLER R. G. Frey
CERVANTES P. E. Russell
CHAUCER George Kane
COPERNICUS Owen Gingerich
DIDEROT Peter France
GEORGE ELIOT Rosemary Ashton
ERASMUS James McConica
GIBBON J. W. Burrow
GODWIN Alan Ryan
GOETHE T. J. Reed
HERZEN Aileen Kelly
JEFFERSON Jack P. Greene
JOHNSON Pat Rogers

LAMARCK L. J. Jordanova
LEIBNIZ G. M. Ross
LINNAEUS W. T. Stearn
LOCKE John Dunn
MENDEL Vitezslav Orel
MILL William Thomas
WILLIAM MORRIS Peter Stansky
MUHAMMAD Michael Cook
THOMAS MORE Anthony Kenny
NEWTON P. M. Rattansi
PETRARCH Nicholas Mann
RUSKIN George P. Landow
SHAKESPEARE Germaine Greer
ADAM SMITH D. D. Raphael
SOCRATES Bernard Williams
VICO Peter Burke

and others

Raymond Williams

COBBETT

Oxford   New York

OXFORD UNIVERSITY PRESS

1983

Oxford University Press, Walton Street, Oxford OX2 6DP

London Glasgow New York Toronto
Delhi Bombay Calcutta Madras Karachi
Kuala Lumpur Singapore Hong Kong Tokyo
Nairobi Dar es Salaam Cape Town
Melbourne Auckland

and associates in
Beirut Berlin Ibadan Mexico City Nicosia

First published 1983 as an Oxford University Press paperback
and simultaneously in a hardback edition

British Library Cataloguing in Publication Data

Williams, Raymond
Cobbett. – (Past Masters)
1. Cobbett, William – Criticism and interpretation
I. Title II. Series
828'.608 PR4461.C/
ISBN 0-19-287576-0
ISBN 0-19-287575-2 Pbk

Library of Congress Cataloging in Publication Data

Williams, Raymond.
Cobbett.
(Past masters)
Bibliography: p.
Includes index.
1. Cobbett, William, 1763 – 1835. 2. Politicians –
Great Britain – Biography. 3. Authors, English –
19th century – Biography. I. Title. II. Series.
DA522.C5W53 1983 941.07'3'0924 [B]. 82-14279
ISBN 0-19-287576-0
ISBN 0-19-287575-2 (pbk)

Set by Datamove Ltd
Printed in Great Britain by
Cox & Wyman Ltd,
Reading

Contents

Abbreviations

Quotations from Cobbett are identified by means of the following abbreviations:

A	*Advice to Young Men*
C	*Cottage Economy*
F	*Eleven Lectures on the French and Belgian Revolutions and English Boroughmongering*
G	*A Grammar of the English Language*
L	*The Life and Letters of William Cobbett*
M	*Manchester Lectures*
O	*The Opinions of William Cobbett*
P	*Life and Adventures of Peter Porcupine*
R	*Rural Rides*
T	*Cobbett's Two-Penny Trash*
W	*Porcupine's Works*

References to *Cobbett's Weekly Political Register* are given by date alone, thus: (10.7.1824). Otherwise the above abbreviations are followed by a reference to the relevant (volume and) page(s) of the work in question, in the edition specified on p. 82, except that *Rural Rides* and *Cobbett's Two-Penny Trash* are referred to by date, thus: (R 30.7.1823), (T 5.1.1831). When a page-reference is given without a preceding abbreviation, the quotation in question comes from the same work as the previous quotation; when no reference at all is given, the reference for the previous quotation applies again.

1 Life

The year is 1822. The place is Sussex, on the south coast of England. The man is William Cobbett.

> When at Battle, I had no intention of going to Lewes, till on the evening of my arrival at Battle, a gentleman ... observed to me that I would do well not to go to Lewes. That very observation made me resolve to go. I went, as a spectator, to the meeting; and I left no one ignorant of the place where I was to be found. I did not covet the noise of a dinner of some 200 to 300 persons; and I did not intend to go to it; but, being pressed to go, I finally went. After some previous common-place occurrences, Mr Kemp, formerly a member for Lewes, was called to the chair; and he having given for a toast, '*the speedy discovery of a remedy for our distresses*,' Mr Ebenezer Johnstone, a gentleman of Lewes, whom I had never seen or heard of until that day, but who, I understand, is a very opulent and most respectable man, proposed *my health*, as that of a person likely to be able to point out the wished-for remedy. – This was the signal for the onset. Immediately upon the toast being given, a Mr Hitchins, a farmer of Seaford, duly prepared for the purpose, got upon the table ... No sooner had Hitchins done, than up started Mr Ingram, a farmer of Rottendean, who was the second person in the drama (for all had been duly prepared) and moved that I should be *put out of the room*! Some few of the Webb Hallites, joined by about six or eight of the dark, dirty-faced, half-whiskered, tax-eaters from Brighton (which is only eight miles off) joined in this cry. I rose, that they might see the man that they had to put out ... (R 9.1.1822)

'That they might see the man.' We can look ourselves, through some contemporary eyes.

Dressed in a blue coat, yellow swansdown waistcoat, drab jersey small-clothes, and top boots ... he was the perfect representation of what he always wished to be – an English gentleman-farmer. (Samuel Bamford)

A very pleasant man: easy of access, affable, clear-headed, simple and mild in his manner, deliberate and unruffled in his speech, though some of his expressions were not very well qualified. His figure is tall and portly; he has a good sensible face, rather full, with little gray eyes, a hard, square forehead, a ruddy complexion, with hair gray or powdered, and had on a scarlet broad-cloth waistcoat, with the flaps of the pockets hanging down, as was the custom for gentlemen-farmers in the last century. (William Hazlitt)

His appearance was prepossessing: a strong, hale, stout man, with a head crowned with the snow of age, a ruddy countenance, a small laughing eye, and the figure of a respectable English farmer. (J. S. Buckingham)

The man two English farmers proposed should be '*put out of the room*!' A man of whom Coleridge said: 'I entertain toward ... Cobbetts ... and all these creatures – and to the Foxites, who have nourished the vipers – a feeling more like hatred than I ever bore to other Flesh and Blood.' A man prosecuted, in 1810, for sedition, and sentenced to two years' imprisonment and to be bound to keep the peace for a further seven years. A man who had to get out of the country, in 1817, and go to the United States, to escape a virtually certain sentence after the suspension of Habeas Corpus. A man who was prosecuted again, in 1831, for incitement and subversion, though the jury were equally divided and the case was dropped. The Clerk to the Privy Council noted: 'His insolence and violence were past endurance, but he made an able speech.' It is not an easy figure to focus. We can try it another way, looking at significant moments in his life, as they came.

1763–82

My father, when I was born, was a farmer ... My first occupation was, driving the small birds from the turnip-seed, and the rooks from the peas. When I first trudged a-field, with my wooden bottle and my satchel swung over my shoulders, I was hardly able to climb the gates and stiles; and, at the close of the day, to reach home, was a task of infinite difficulty. My next employment was weeding wheat, and leading a single horse at harrowing barley. Hoeing peas followed, and hence, I arrived at the honour of joining the reapers in harvest, driving the team, and holding plough ... Our religion was that of the Church of England ... As to politics, we were like the rest of the country people in England; that is to say, we neither knew nor thought any thing about the matter ... After, however, the American war had continued for some time ... my father was a partizan of the Americans ... He who pleaded the cause of the Americans, had an advantage, too, with young minds: he had only to represent the king's troops as sent to cut the throats of a people, our friends and relations, merely because they would not submit to oppression; and his cause was gained. Speaking to the passions, is ever sure to succeed on the uninformed ... He continued an American, and so staunch a one, that he would not have suffered his best friend to drink success to the king's arms at his table ... Whether he was right or wrong, is not now worth talking about: that I had no opinion of my own is certain; for, had my father been on the other side, I should have been on the other side too; and should have looked upon the company I then made a part of as malcontents and rebels. (P 20–4)

1782

I, for the first time, beheld the sea, and no sooner did I behold it, than I wished to be a sailor ... But it was not the sea alone that I saw: the grand fleet was riding at anchor in Spithead ... I had heard talk of the glorious deeds of our admirals and sailors, of the defeat of the Spanish Armada, and of all those memorable combats, that good and true Englishmen never fail to relate to their children about a hundred times a year ... My heart was inflated with national pride. The sailors

were my countrymen; the fleet belonged to my country, and
surely I had my part in it ... The Captain ... persuaded me
to return home, and I remember he concluded his advice, with
telling me, that it was better to be led to church in a halter, to
be tied to a girl that I did not like, than to be tied to the gang-
way, or, as the sailors call it, married to *miss roper*. From the
conclusion of this wholesome counsel, I perceived that the
Captain thought I had eloped on account of a bastard. I
blushed ... I returned once more to the plough, but I was
spoiled for a farmer. (24–6)

1783

Cobbett left home for London, on a sudden impulse. He was
then just short of his twentieth birthday. He had made these
impulsive moves before, and not only when looking at the fleet.
At fourteen he had gone to work in the Bishop of Winchester's
garden, in his home town of Farnham in Surrey. A gardener
told him of the beauties of the King's Gardens in Kew. Cobbett
walked there the next day. He spent his last pence on a copy of
Swift's *Tale of a Tub*, and read it overnight in a haystack, where
he also slept. He got work at Kew, sweeping leaves. He was
wearing a blue smock, red garters, hide shoes. Three boys of
about his age came by, and laughed at his dress. The young
Cobbett looked back at lace ruffles, silk stockings and buckled
shoes. They were George Prince of Wales and his brothers. His
father found out where he was and fetched him home to
Farnham.

The move at twenty was more decisive, though unplanned. He
eventually got work as an attorney's clerk in Gray's Inn.

The office (for so the dungeon where I wrote was called) was
so dark, that, on cloudy days, we were obliged to burn candle.
I worked like a galley-slave from five in the morning till eight
or nine at night ... When I think of the *saids* and *soforths*,
and the counts of tautology that I scribbled over; when I think
of those sheets of seventy-two words, and those lines two
inches apart, my brain turns. (30)

1784–91

After seeing an advertisement, Cobbett decided to enlist in the Royal Marines, but took the shilling, by error, into a marching regiment. During his first year in the army, on top of his drills, he read in a circulating library and studied grammar: 'I wrote the whole grammar out two or three times; I got it by heart; I repeated it every morning and every evening, and, when on guard, I imposed on myself the task of saying it all over once every time I was posted sentinel' (34). He was made corporal. The regiment was in Nova Scotia, Canada. Early in 1785 he was sent with a detachment to join it. He became clerk to the regiment, and within a year sergeant-major. Six feet one inch in his stockings, 'I was *always ready* ... never did any man, or anything, wait one moment for me' (A 40). His position

> brought me in close contact, at every hour, with the whole of the *Epaulet* gentry, whose profound and surprising ignorance I discovered in a twinkling. But, I had a very delicate part to act with these gentry; for, while I despised them for their gross ignorance and their vanity, and hated them for their drunkenness and rapacity, I was fully sensible of *their power* ... (6.12.1817)

When the regiment returned to England in late 1791, and after he had been granted honourable discharge, Cobbett wrote to the Secretary at War, making detailed charges of corruption and peculation against four named officers of the regiment.

1792

While we follow the life of this single man we can temporarily forget the significance of the dates now inscribed. The French Revolution had begun in 1789, while he was in Canada. Its effects were strongly felt in England, and there was violent controversy between its radical sympathisers and its determined opponents. Among the flying publications there was a short pamphlet, *The Soldier's Friend*, stating the grievances of English soldiers and proposing redress. In 1805 Cobbett denied that he had written it. In 1832 he said that it was 'the very first thing I ever wrote for the press in my life' (23.6.1832). It certainly overlaps in content the formal charges he had made against his four former officers.

There is then a period which is not easy to interpret. A key witness in the proposed court martial of the officers was refused his discharge. The War Office failed to secure the regimental books on which the charges depended. The indictment, Cobbett said, was only partially drawn. Witnesses were to be produced that Cobbett had 'drunk to the destruction of the house of Brunswick'. This in 1792, after the people of Paris had marched on Versailles and brought the French royal family back to Paris.

In February Cobbett married Ann Reid, whom he had met as a daughter of a sergeant of artillery in a neighbouring regiment in Canada. In March the court martial was convened and Cobbett did not appear. After an adjournment the officers were acquitted. Cobbett was on his way to France.

He lived near St Omer for nearly six months: 'the six happiest months of my life', he wrote four years later (P 39). But there is then a problem of the relation between what he thought at the time — for he had chosen to go to France *after* the Revolution — and what he later says he thought.

I found the people, among whom I lived, excepting those who were already blasted with the principles of the accursed revolution, honest, pious, and kind to excess. People may say what they please about the misery of the French peasantry, under the old government; I have conversed with thousands of them, not ten among whom did not regret the change. I have not room here to go into an inquiry into the causes that have led these people to become the passive instruments, the slaves of a set of tyrants such as the world never saw before, but I venture to predict, that, sooner or later, they will return to that form of government under which they were happy and under which alone they can ever be so again. (39–40)

However this may be, Cobbett was on his way to Paris when he heard, at Abbeville, that the Tuileries had been attacked and the king deposed. He turned off to the nearest port from which he could sail for America, where he arrived, in New York, in October.

> My determination to settle in the United States was formed before I went to France, and even before I quitted the army. A desire of seeing a country ... of which I had heard and read so much ... above all, an inclination for seeing the world, led me to this determination ... I had imbibed principles of republicanism ... I was ambitious to become a citizen of a free state ... I thought that men enjoyed here a greater degree of liberty than in England; and this, if not the principal reason, was at least one, for my coming to this country. (40)

1792–1800

The difficulty of understanding Cobbett, in that crucial year 1792, increases when we compare the work he did in the next seven and a half years, in the republican United States, with the work he eventually did when he returned to royalist England. His modern radical admirers are often uneasy about this Cobbett of the 1790s. His fierce pamphleteering, from what is by any standards the political Right, is acknowledged but then moved on from. It requires a closer look.

His first intervention was an attack on the addresses of welcome to Joseph Priestley when he arrived in the United States, and through these on Priestley himself. Chemist, discoverer of oxygen, dissenting minister and friend of the American and French revolutions, Priestley arrived in New York in 1794, and declined both a professorship and a ministry. His house and laboratory had been burned by a 'Church and King' crowd in Birmingham in 1791. Cobbett wrote: 'He was himself the principal cause of these riots ... The rioters did nothing that was not perfectly consonant to the principles he had for many years been labouring to infuse into their minds' (W I 159). Priestley, he argued, instead of being welcomed should be plainly seen as an infidel and a rabble-rouser. First a Deist and then a Unitarian, he was one of those who 'always introduce their political claims and projects under the mask of religion ... He beat his drum ecclesiastic to raise recruits to the cause of rebellion' (153). Such men 'flatter and inflame the lower orders of the people' (170). 'The same visionary delusion seems to have pervaded reformers in all ages. They do not consider what *can* be done, but what they think ought to be done' (169). This particular 'visionary delusion' was the reform of the British parliament. But 'system-mongers are an unreasonable species of mortals; place, climate, nature itself must give way; they must have the same government in every quarter of the globe' (172). Fortunately the people did not want reform.

> If the English chose to remain slaves, bigots and idolaters, as the Doctor calls them, that was no business of his ... he should have let them alone ... But no, said the Doctor, I will reform you — I will enlighten you — I will make you free. You shall not, say the people. But I will! says the Doctor. By —, say the people, you shall not. (177)

As for the burning of his house, was he not a friend of the French Revolution, where there had been killing and destruction on so great a scale that 'the mind turns for relief and consolation to the riot at Birmingham' (159)?

In a subsequent series of pamphlets, Cobbett continued to attack ideas of democratic reform, especially in England, through what he saw as their regular association with religious and personal infidelity and above all with the atrocities committed in the name of liberty in the French Revolution. 'At the very name of democrat, humanity shudders, and modesty hides its head' (W II 131). This is from *A Bone to Gnaw for the Democrats*, a pamphlet mainly concerned with the bloody events in France. Cobbett is an effective narrator, but also a master of guilt by association. Rousseau, for example, with his 'eternal cant about *virtue* and *liberty*, seems to have assumed the mask of virtue for no other purpose than that of propagating with more certain success the blackest and most incorrigible vice' (W III 176). Paine — 'mad Tom' — was not only an infidel but showed his true character in his second marriage; he was thus 'made for a French republican: the baseness which they have constantly discovered is in your nature' (W IV 326). This was a general characteristic of such reformers: 'They are all citizens of the world; country, and friends and relations, are unworthy the attention of men who are occupied in rendering all mankind free and happy' (W IV 79). It was difficult to find a democrat or rebel who was not also a bad husband, father, brother or son. Thus Paine was not only 'the prince of demagogues' but 'infamous', an 'old ruffian', a 'poor, mean-spirited miscreant' and a 'vile wretch'. The politics are seen to follow from such characteristics.

Such attacks on Priestley, Paine and later the American doctor Rush (who got heavy damages against him) stand out from these years of pamphleteering but do not indicate their whole tenor. His fierce opposition to the bloody course of the revolution in France is relatively carefully documented. His interventions in the complicated political relations between the United States, France and England, and in the internal American controversy between Federalists and anti-Federalists, are often slashing but are usually also argued and sustained. His most consistent position is an absolute loyalty to his idea of England, where in fact, in the fifteen years before his return in 1800, he had spent just four months.

1801–6

Cobbett was welcomed back to England by the whole anti-Jacobin party and by leaders of the Government, including Pitt. He was offered control of one of the two Government newspapers, but refused. He said he would make his own way. Meanwhile he collected his American writings, in twelve volumes, and the subscription list was headed by the Prince of Wales (who had laughed at him as a boy in Kew Gardens) and six other 'royal highnesses'. The dedication was to the founder of a 'Loyal Association against Republicans and Levellers', and Cobbett, in an introduction, declared himself against 'the Licentious Politics and the Infidel Philosophy of the Present Age'. Republicanism and rebellion had been nourished by the success of the American revolution, with especially damaging effects in Ireland. The French Revolution, with its 'two millions of persons murdered', showed the reality of the talk about 'liberty' and 'democracy'. 'And is there — can there be, a faction . . . so cruel — so bloody minded, as to wish to see these scenes repeated in their own, or any other country? If there be — Great God . . . sweep the sanguinary race from the face of the Creation!!!' (W II 132).

This is downright enough. But what we have now to look at is one of the most extraordinary shifts in the history of political writing. Here is a man rising forty, with a reputation on both sides of the Atlantic as one of the most vigorous, indeed virulent, anti-democratic journalists. Within five years he is a radical; within ten in gaol for sedition. How is this change to be understood?

Shifts the other way are very common, as young radicals turn conservative in middle age or with settlement and success. The key to Cobbett's shift may be that he was at last in close contact with the country and political system which he had been idealising, in absence, for so many years. He was continually to refer to the happier England of his boyhood, before this long absence. Yet the shift had several phases. First, he opposed the Peace of Amiens, and had his house attacked by 'a base and hireling mob', 'a blood-thirsty rabble' (L I 133–5), because he refused to illuminate it in celebration. (And he had not been labouring for many years to infuse the principles of riot into their minds.)

In 1802 Cobbett had begun publication of the *Political Register*, which, mainly as a weekly paper, was to go on appearing until his death in 1835. An earlier journalistic attempt, at a daily paper called *Porcupine* — intended to show 'the injurious and degrading consequences of discontent, disloyalty, and innovation' — had failed financially, under the weight of general pressure by the government against an independent press. Cobbett's *Political Register*, through which the shift in his opinions became public and influential, made some genuine innovations in style, notably in separating what would now be called the 'leading article' — an opinion or argument — from the reporting of news. Cobbett also developed the important late-eighteenth-century form of the Open Letter, which, as a form, is an exact expression of the political transition then occurring: from attempts at private influence, in correspondence within a ruling class to persons in power, to attempts at public influence, within the same limited circle, by a quasi-personal form of address. Earlier developments (as in the famous Letters of Junius, 1772), had first broken and then adapted the convention of privacy. Cobbett, with his taste for *ad hominem* argument, widened and finally broke the political 'circle' altogether. He was later to make the same breakthrough by establishing the publication of parliamentary debates (which had long been resisted) and in effect beginning what is now the official and apparently 'traditional' Hansard.

The war was resumed in 1803, and Cobbett was happy with it. Yet a deeper shift was now beginning. As a reward for writing on the Government's side, Cobbett was offered a 'slice' of a loan:

> As the *scrip* ... was always directly at a *premium*, a bargain was always made with the loan-monger that he should admit certain favourites of the Government to have certain portions of *scrip* at the same price that he gave for it. I was offered such a portion of *scrip*, which, as I was told, would put a hundred or two pounds into my pocket at once ... I soon found that the *scrip* was never even to be shown to me, and that I had merely to pocket the amount of the *premium*. I refused to have anything to do with the matter, for which I got heartily laughed at. (M IV)

This characteristically sharp offer was made to a man who had first entered public life as an enemy of financial corruption. It was its accepted character, among his anti-democratic political friends, that shocked him. He began studying the financial system, drawing heavily on a book by Paine which he had earlier dismissed. Within months he was attacking the manipulators of loans, funds and stocks, 'all the innumerable swarm of locusts, who, without stirring ten miles from the capital, devour three fourths of the produce of the whole land'(21.5.1803). The mode of exaggeration was persistent, but a new and central theme of Cobbett's life had been decisively introduced.

In 1805 the next shift was determined. After twenty years living in towns or army barracks, he bought a farm, Fairthorn, in the village of Botley near Southampton. He became closely involved in bringing up his family, on which he had 'always admired the sentiment of Rousseau' (A 281). A neighbouring common, Horton Heath, was the subject of a proposal for enclosure. Cobbett campaigned against this and all similar proposals, and aligned them with the substitution of annual tenancies for leases, and with the new pressures of rack-renting and land speculation and engrossment. He aligned this whole economic process, in turn, with the new financial system, which had 'drawn the real property of the nation into fewer hands ... made land and agriculture objects of speculation ... in every part of the kingdom, moulded many farms into one ... almost entirely extinguished the race of small farmers ... We are daily advancing to the state in which there are but two classes of men, *masters*, and *abject dependants*' (15.3.1806). The farmer's son who had become a soldier and then a patriotic political pamphleteer had come back to his own land and was redefining his patriotism. Not that he would yet admit to anything but the most scrupulous consistency.

Further stages now rapidly followed. His proposals for army reform, to end the exploitation of private soldiers, were ignored by his political friends. His opposition to corruption in parliamentary elections, including the open buying of votes, led him to intervene in by-elections, though still 'of what has been denominated Parliamentary Reform, I have always disapproved ... Of universal suffrage I have witnessed the defects too attentively and with too much disgust ever to think of it with approbation' (15.3.1806). Yet, in the continuing war with France, a new point of contrast had to be made: 'France ... has exhibited a most complete proof of what *the people alone* are able to do' (6.12.1806). Meanwhile the English political system had shown him, in spite of all his feelings 'on the side of birth and rank', that there was a systematic combination 'against the exercise of the undoubted rights of the people', and that this was based on 'the arrogant and unjust allegation, that, on account of our low birth, we were unworthy of any public influence or trust'. The most important word in that sentence is *we*. At the age of forty-three, after the long detour from the mood of the indignant honest soldier against the '*Epaulet* gentry', after the fierce polemics against what were seen as alien beliefs and institutions, he was again in his own country with his own people, saying 'we' defiantly against a system of arrogance and corruption, which he might appear to have served, against its foreign enemies, but which he would nevertheless, when invited, not join. His real class position was now disclosed in the general condition of the majority of his fellow-countrymen, and with that his new enemies.

The general shift is decisive, but within it certain elements persist. There are habits of simple abusiveness and aggression, which often precede their focus. There are persistent prejudices against those he can see as an alien group (unbelievers, blacks, Jews). There is the generally conservative cast of mind in matters of social custom and observance. There is also, though the causes may change, the quick, often reckless courage, and the willingness to defy both authority and public opinion. These, within the historical shift which decisively remade the political writer, remain as the personal continuities of Cobbett.

1809–12

In June 1809, in the cathedral city of Ely, the local English militia protested that the price of their knapsacks was being deducted from their pay. They surrounded their officers and demanded the money due to them. This was taken to be mutiny. Four squadrons of German mercenary soldiers, stationed at Bury St Edmunds, were brought in to suppress it. Five of the English militia were tried and sentenced to five hundred lashes each. Part of this brutal sentence was carried out.

Cobbett moved in on one of his central concerns: the dishonest and cruel treatment of common soldiers. It was said of Napoleon's army that they were often chained and lashed so that they would not rise against the tyrant they hated. What then of this flogging at Ely? What could be said now that 'our "gallant defenders" not only require physical restraint, in certain cases, but even a little blood drawn from their backs, and that too, with the aid and assistance of German troops' (1.7.1809)? Again:

> Well done, Lord Castlereagh! This is just what it was thought your plan would produce. Well said, Mr Huskisson! It really was not without reason that you dwelt, with so much earnestness, upon the great utility of the foreign troops ... *Five hundred lashes each*! ... What! mutiny for the *price of a knapsack*? Lash them! flog them!

Upon reading this, the Attorney-General filed an information against Cobbett for sedition.

It was a time of many repressive trials. A radical surgeon, Gale Jones, was imprisoned by the House of Commons for 'breach of privilege'. The protest of Francis Burdett, a leading reformer, against this sentence, brought a Speaker's warrant for his own imprisonment in the Tower. Crowds gathered around Burdett's house. The Government called in all soldiers stationed within a hundred miles of London. The City police ordered them away. There was talk of a general rising, but the soldiers rushed the house and took Burdett to the Tower. Cobbett's trial, delayed for various reasons (an information was often laid to intimidate, without the need for trial), came up ten weeks later.

He was resolved to defend himself, on the model of Horne Tooke in the notorious treason trials of 1794. He based much of his defence on directly comparable remarks made in the House of Commons. The judge, Ellenborough, ruled out this evidence as 'privileged'. Cobbett lost his way in the argument. The judge was openly against him. Most juries of this sort were packed. After five minutes' retirement, he was found guilty, and sentenced to two years in Newgate gaol. He smiled when he was sentenced.

It was part of the system of privilege that a prisoner with

money could buy himself out of the pestilential conditions of the common gaol. For twelve guineas a week Cobbett hired part of the head gaoler's lodgings; had his own food sent in; had friends to visit and members of his family to stay. But this expense was on top of the fine and costs of six thousand pounds, and meant probable financial ruin. He was helped by friends, but it was a hard and complicated time. Yet from Newgate gaol he not only organised his children's education (there were a daughter and four sons; a first-born had died and a second was born dead) and, at a distance, the work of his farm, but mounted vigorous new political campaigns in the *Register*. These included many articles on the crisis of the banking and funding system; early interventions on the Luddite disturbances, which he traced to widespread unemployment and the high price of bread ('measures ought to be adopted, not so much for putting an end to riots, as to prevent the misery out of which they arise', 23.11.1811); and a characteristic response to the assassination of the Prime Minister, Perceval, in which he reviewed his political record and insisted that most people were glad about his death; even his private funeral had to be guarded by soldiers. When martial law was declared, in 1811, he seized on the case of a Manchester woman who had been hanged for '*highway robbery*' after taking some potatoes out of a cart. To the Government assertions of treasonable conspiracy, Cobbett replied: 'They can find no *agitators*. It is a movement of the *people's own*' (25.7.1812).

During these years of widespread disturbance, Cobbett in gaol was as powerful as if at liberty; as politically powerful, though still in serious financial trouble. When he was at last released, six hundred of his radical friends gave him a dinner in London. On his way back to his farm in Hampshire the church bells were rung in towns and villages as he passed through, and he was cheered triumphantly home.

1816–17

The war against France ended in 1815. 'The play is over,' wrote a Government paper, 'we may now go to supper.' Cobbett replied: 'No, *you cannot yet go to supper*. You have not yet *paid for the play*. And, before you have paid for the play, you will find that there is no money left for the supper' (23.10.1816). He was obviously right. These were to be years of very great distress. Unemployment spread rapidly. Wages were reduced and working hours lengthened. The burden of direct and indirect taxation was heavy. Agriculture was widely disrupted, and many farms went bankrupt.

In the years since his release from gaol Cobbett had continued his campaigns, but there were disputes inside the radical movement to add to its external difficulties. Now, with the war over, renewal was possible, and especially in the campaign for parliamentary reform. Yet this political campaign found itself in the middle of a major social and economic crisis. Within these urgent developments, Cobbett came, in effect, to change his constituency, his audience. Beyond the general radical appeal to all those who were not the actual agents and beneficiaries of the system of corruption, exploitation and repression, he now began to address himself directly to 'the Journeymen and Labourers', in a new twopenny *Register*.

Through various devices of publication, and against several kinds of repression and fraud, he succeeded in creating an almost unprecedented popular circulation, rising to between forty and fifty thousand a week, much higher than that of any other journal. (A popular public of this size had not been regularly reached before, though for occasional publications, such as Paine's *Rights of Man* in the early 1790s, or Cobbett's own separate publications in this period, even higher figures were reached.) This regular readership was in itself a form of political organisation, and Cobbett proved to be jealous of alternative radical forms, such as the Hampden Clubs.

At the centre of Cobbett's arguments, in this period, was the priority of parliamentary reform, to which, after so much early opposition, he was to remain devoted. This was to be accomplished by annual elections to the Commons and the extension of the vote to all who paid *direct* taxation. Cobbett defended this limited extension of the vote by a rhetorical flourish against the enfranchisement of 'mere menial servants, vagrants, pickpockets and scamps of all sorts' (2.11.1816). This conveniently omitted the great body of working people and labourers, who were the principal sufferers from the general crisis and whom he had chosen as his specific audience. There is thus still a paradox, of a kind which became general and decisive in the whole period leading to parliamentary reform in 1832 and beyond. A general popular movement was raised in the interest of a reform which would exclude most of its supporters. It can be put more harshly: this intense phase of self-organisation and protest by a still-forming working and labouring class was intervened in and in part appropriated by a primarily middle-class reforming movement, in the interest of small employers.

Cobbett's influential *Address to the Journeymen and Labourers* (2.11.1816) is a model of this position. He begins by conceding the emerging working-class claim that 'the real strength and all the resources of a country, ever have sprung and ever must spring, from the *labour* of its people'. He acknowledges 'with what indignation must you hear yourselves called the Populace, the Rabble, the Mob, the Swinish Multitude'. But 'suppress your indignation', until the causes have been explained: 'It is the lot of mankind, that some shall labour with their limbs and others with their minds; and, on all occasions ... it is the duty of the latter to come to the assistance of the former.' With this candid assertion of the permanence of this fundamental division of labour within class society, Cobbett establishes a specific relation to his new popular audience. The remedies of the ruling class are cruel and deceptive, but the people's own uninstructed responses can be dangerous. Indeed 'we want *great alteration*, but we want *nothing new*'.

Cobbett was often subsequently to cite these arguments as proof that he had always been on the side of orderly reform as against popular disorder. His own position was again to change, but it is an instructive irony that when he made this defence it usually did him no good.

Theoretically the positions can be distinguished and have to be distinguished. But historically it was their *conjunction*, for

all the blurring and paradox, which alarmed the ruling class.
Cobbett wanted a reformed parliament to reduce direct taxation
so that employers might provide more and better-paid jobs.
Heavy taxation now went to support a corrupt establishment
and army. Popular resentment of this should, however, be
channelled towards the restoration of ordinary fair employment, with this monstrous tax-eating aristocratic head cut off
(though that fierce image should not be used; annual election
and the taxpayer's vote would have the same effect, gently and
simply).

Yet in those critical years it made little difference whether the
talk was rational or desperate, gentle or wild. The effect was the
same: a growing threat to a corrupt and cruel aristocratic State.
Plots and conspiracies; spies and provocateurs; pamphlets and
meetings: all swirled indistinguishably in the panic of that State.
A newspaper here, a machine-breaking there, a meeting, a
riotous assembly: the differences mattered little, within the perceived combined threat. Habeas Corpus was again suspended;
public meetings and reading-rooms controlled; 'agitators' made
liable to imprisonment without trial. Cobbett was offered a
government bribe to stop writing. When that offer came, and
fearing arrest if he refused it, he again left England and sailed to
the United States, arriving in May 1817.

1819–20

Cobbett's second period of residence in the United States
proved to be exceptionally productive in a new, or at least
developed, kind of writing. The *Register* was continued in
England, and he went on contributing to it. But he came to write
more broadly, in what became four books. His *History of the
Last Hundred Days of English Freedom* grew directly from the
crisis from which he had temporarily escaped. *A Year's Residence in the United States of America* introduced a new mode,
by which he is now centrally remembered: a unique combination
of social and political argument with detailed observation of
a varied way of life. *The American Gardener*, later rewritten
as *The English Gardener*, was another new kind of book,

combining detailed practical instruction with wide observation and, again, social commentary. There was also the remarkable *Grammar of the English Language*, written in letter form as an instrument of popular education, and characteristically using current political events in the grammatical examples: 'Sidmouth *writes* a Circular Letter; Sidmouth *wrote* a Circular Letter; Sidmouth *will write* a Circular Letter' (G 255). The illustrated array of tenses is also the continuity of the tyrannical Home Secretary.

There is a problem of perspective. Cobbett is now better known as the author of these books, written while he was away from the centre of the struggle, than for his active part in the struggle, which continued to preoccupy him. Certainly the books, or parts of them, outlive the events of the day, but many of their qualities — the vigorous plain style, the variety of interest, the sense of an engaged and irrepressible personality — are the direct consequence of the struggle itself. Cobbett wrote the books, but also these years of exposure and practice wrote Cobbett.

In May 1819 his house in New York State was destroyed by fire. In the following October he sailed for England. An extra-ordinary few months were to follow.

He landed at Liverpool on board the *Hercules* on 22 November 1819. A large crowd gathered at the docks to greet him, and he announced a public meeting for 24 November. At this meeting he was presented with Addresses from many other towns, including Manchester. A hundred days earlier, on St Peter's Fields, Manchester, at least eleven people had been killed, and more than five hundred injured, by a Yeomanry charge with sabres on a peaceful meeting of some sixty thousand people, in favour of parliamentary reform. Cobbett was invited to go on to Manchester to speak, and accepted. On his way there, at Irlam, he received a letter from the borough-reeves and constables of Manchester and Salford warning him against any public entry. He replied in one of his most spirited letters:

Is it really come to this, that a man upon returning to his country, or upon moving from one part of England to

another, is to be stopped on his way by threats of interference
on the part of officers appointed to keep the peace? . . . Is it
really come to this? Is this the state of England? Is this the
law? . . . To what a pitch must men have arrived, when they
could sit down and look at one another in the face, while they
wrote and signed a paper such as that you sent me . . . I dis-
dain to tell you what my intentions are, whether I intend to
enter Manchester or not. (L II 119–21)

But he did not go on to Manchester. He went to Coventry and
then to London, to further large meetings.

One strange element ran through these difficult days. In 1796
he had attacked the 'infamous Tom Paine'. He had concluded
with these words:

How Tom gets a living now, or what brothel he inhabits, I
know not, nor does it much signify to any body here or any-
where else. He has done all the mischief he can in the world,
and whether his carcass is at last to be suffered to rot on the
earth, or to be dried in the air, is of very little consequence.
Whenever or wherever he breathes his last, he will excite
neither sorrow nor compassion; no friendly hand will close
his eyes, not a groan will be uttered, not a tear will be shed.
Like *Judas* he will be remembered by posterity; men will learn
to express all that is base, malignant, treacherous, unnatural
and blasphemous, by the single monosyllable, Paine. (W IV
112–13)

Since this terrible expression of calculated abuse, Cobbett had
read and learned much from Paine's *Decline and Fall of the
English System of Finance*. He now discovered that Paine, as a
Deist, had been refused burial in consecrated ground in
America, and had been buried in a corner of his New Rochelle
farm. It is difficult to know which is the more extraordinary, the
published abuse or what Cobbett now did:

I have done myself the honour to disinter his bones . . . I have
dug them up; they are now on their way to England. When I
myself return, I shall cause them to speak the common sense

of the great man; I shall gather together the people of
Liverpool and Manchester in one assembly with those of
London, and those bones will effect the reformation of
England in Church and State. (L II 116)

Whatever his real hopes, the effect was very different. Hardly
anyone would subscribe to a monument, and in fact he kept
Paine's bones until his own death. Byron's squib was one of
many:

> In digging up your bones, Tom Paine,
> Will Cobbett has done well;
> You visit him on earth again,
> He'll visit you in hell.

Again, from a less skilful hand:

> Why didst thou on the billows toss,
> Or why thy native country fled,
> Why thou the vast Atlantic cross?
> Why, caitiff thief! to rob the dead.
> Lay by thy pen, cork up thine ink,
> None read thee now but drivelling drones,
> Thy boasted fame will end in stink,
> So give me back my pilfered bones.

These lines remind us of what we often forget when we look
back at a vigorously controversial writer: that the blows were
traded both ways. Cobbett certainly got more than his share,
but this is no case for defensive anxiety. As he put it, in general,
later: 'the very way in which I have always proceeded, giving
three, four, or ten blows for one; and never, in any case, ceased
to pursue the assailant, in some way or other, until he was
completely down' (O 45). This is neither literally true, nor, as an
aspiration, very attractive. But what Cobbett was facing in 1819
was more than jokes about Paine's bones; he was facing the
hastily passed and extensively repressive Six Acts.

This set of measures, ranging from summary trials to controls
on meetings, included a severe extension of tax to just the
cheap popular writing on which Cobbett depended. A vicious

combination of legal and financial pressures was brought to bear, specifically, on the radical press. For the rest of his life Cobbett was to be involved, with many others – including some, like the radical publishers and journalists Carlile (*The Black Dwarf*), Wooler and Hetherington, who defied the pressures more directly – in the struggle against the 'taxes on knowledge'; a struggle through which a relative freedom of the Press in Britain was eventually won. But the immediate consequences were severe. Hard pressed by this and other financial troubles, Cobbett went bankrupt, and among other things lost his farm and woodland at Botley, which he had owned since 1805.

1821

Cobbett's life after his loss of the farm at Botley can be seen as a series of campaigns and publications, as indeed can his earlier life from the end of his army service onwards. Such a record is just, but it lacks a dimension which is of substantial importance. Born on a farm, and doing farm and garden work until he ran away to London just before he was twenty, Cobbett, after he had settled again in England, never for long kept away from some kind of country work, but at the same time usually attempted to combine it with other kinds of work, notably an increasingly metropolitan politics and publishing. This means that we have to think in a special way about 'Cobbett the countryman'. That he was a countryman not only 'born and bred' but in one way or another for two-thirds of his working life is not in doubt; yet to say that he was only a countryman, intervening from that position in politics and publishing, would be very misleading.

The point has some general importance. Two other writers whom we think of, with Cobbett, as among our leading writers on country life, have the same mixed relationship to it. Arthur Young of the great *Annals of Agriculture* (1784–1809) was born into a merchant-financed estate, failed as a small farmer, succeeded as an agricultural journalist and pioneer of new farming knowledge. In a later generation Richard Jefferies, son of a small farmer who failed and became a jobbing gardener, earned his living as a journalist and author. In their very different ways, Young, Cobbett and Jefferies directly experienced the crisis of the rural economy in the period in which it was ceasing to be central or dominant. What they then wrote, again for all their individual differences, is thus never 'rural writing' in a simple sense. In their work, as in their lives, what counted was the interaction of the inherited rural ways with new and very powerful social, economic and technical forces.

Cobbett's base from 1821 expresses this relationship and this material more clearly than in any earlier period. Botley had been an attempt at a large farm or small estate, financed by his London writing. He had workers and servants and many guests; he planted trees, mowed lawns, encouraged field sports and fist fights, improved his land and his gardens. His initial plan was to move from Botley, except on occasional business, for the three winter months only. The ideal at least, and often the reality, belong to an eighteenth-century tradition of the country estate which is partly self-supporting (and cheap, and provides good food) and yet is both purchased and financed by some kind of urban or merchant trade.

Cobbett's new place at Kensington, after the bankruptcy, is significantly different. Most obviously it is much nearer the metropolis on which the politics and the publishing have mainly to be based. More particularly it is a combination of smallholding – 'four acres of rich land for cows and pigs' – and nursery garden. From this base Cobbett then developed a seedfarm, starting with the import of American maize and the new 'swede' turnips, which he popularised in his journalism. He also sold nursery trees, especially his favourite acacias, and for a time meat. His selling and propagation of journals and books fitted, in new ways, with this active and many-sided commercial enterprise. Much of his country writing, including *Cottage Economy* and *The English Gardener* as well as pamphlets and articles in the *Register*, interacts directly with the other enterprises.

The new kind of base had its own financial problems, but in general it was a very successful adaptation to new conditions.

Cobbett never quite gave up the earlier ideal of an estate to pass to his children. In 1831 he acquired a farm, on long lease, near his birthplace, and gave up the Kensington seed-farm, though continuing a seed business. In fact he died relatively poor.

Yet it was the writing and campaigning, from the commercial base at Kensington, that really succeeded and that survived him. *Cottage Economy* (1822) is a central example. It chimes with his political campaigning, in its address to labouring families and in its intention to provide for a healthy and hard-working independence. At the same time the writing and his own developing practice continually interacted. At Botley he had bought in beer and served wine to his guests. Now he is both developing and recommending home-brewing. It is the same with cows, pigs, poultry, goats, straw-plaiting and maize ('Cobbett's Corn'). In much of this Cobbett had lifelong experience, but there is now a new emphasis. It is at once a consciously examined renewal of the elements of a subsistence economy, and yet in the practice and in the writing an enterprise beyond subsistence.

Cobbett is a marvellous instructor in practical matters, not only because his writing is clear and tactile but also because he is often describing what he has just been doing or learning to do. There is an amusing instance in the chapters on baking bread. At first this is all persuasive recommendation of the quality of the product, with nothing about the process. 'It would be shocking indeed if that had to be taught by the means of books' (C 59) though that had not restrained him on beer. By the next chapter, and on real demand, he has got a recipe and instructions from his wife, and is also describing a new flour-mill he is just trying. It is this interactive practice, at times only reached after a certain amount of bluff and bluster, that is Cobbett's real importance as a writer and political figure, and it is at its most important, from his Kensington base, in the 1820s.

There is the same essential quality in the famous *Rural Rides*, which began in 1821 and were published in collection in 1830. Cobbett was now riding out on business, whether in politics or in one of his commercial enterprises. He wanted to look and learn, for every practical reason. Thus the whole man, with whole interests, is engaged at every turn: the politics, the prices, the methods of cultivation and breeding, the look of the people and the houses, the weather and the seasons, the meetings and the conversations, the histories and the changes – all are learned and told in what seems and often literally is a form of two-way writing, which not only in its opinions but in its most basic method is a radical journalism (very different from the 'journalism' of the one-way 'reporter').

The point can be put another way. Cobbett's *History of the Protestant Reformation* (1824 and 1827) belongs to this decade but for all its polemical vigour is without its central qualities. The vigour on its own – plain style, name-calling, broad assertion, personal display – could evolve into a quite different and much lower dimension of 'popular' writing: a way of writing *to* or *at* 'the people', with effect. There are innumerable petty successors of Cobbett in this isolable style, though an increasing number are wholly without his conscience. But at its best, in *Cottage Economy* and the *Rural Rides*, there is a higher definition and dimension of the 'popular': a writing and talking *with* people and current events; an involved observing and learning; a simultaneously engaged and open practicality of address. It is the Cobbett who was in these ways central in his own time who has survived to ours.

1830–2

Cobbett had joined in many political campaigns in the 1820s: in the curious and agitated defence of Queen Caroline against her exclusion by George IV; in the more important campaign for reform of the Combination Acts which were repressing working-class organisations and unions; in the cause of Catholic emancipation (linked with a campaign against poverty in Ireland); in agitation against the Game Laws and the cruel sentencing used to enforce them; in an attack on road tolls through the turnpike trusts; and, characteristically, in attacks on new statutory bodies with local rating powers, such as that proposed to light Newbury with gas. He also stood for the unreformed Parliament, at Coventry and at Preston, but was not elected.

Then in 1830 two major things happened. Within a renewed economic crisis the movement for parliamentary reform became very much stronger, especially in London and the industrial cities and towns; and in the autumn, in the rural counties least affected by neighbouring industrial development, the country labourers began destroying the threshing and other machines which were creating unemployment, and burning the barns and ricks and even the houses of those who would not relieve their extreme distress: parsons who would not reduce tithes; land-lords who kept up rents; farmers who would not raise wages.

Cobbett joined vigorously in both struggles, but with special authority on what he called the 'Rural War'. He had warned so often that it would come to this:

> I knew that English labourers would not lie down and die in any number, with but sour sorrel in their bellies ... I knew that all the palaver in the world, all the wheedling, coaxing, praying; I knew that all the blustering and threatening; I knew that all the teachings of the Tract societies; that all the imprisoning, whipping, and harnessing to carts and wagons; I knew that all these would fail to persuade the honest, sensible and industrious English labourer, that he had not an *indefeas-ible right* to live. (13.11.1830)

Cobbett did not advocate or support the burnings; he wanted to channel the protest towards the parliamentary reform move-ment. But he was indignant that the military were sent in against these starving and desperate fellow-countrymen. Moreover, with typical bluntness, he recognised what the fires were doing to the cold indifference of the rich and powerful. Even while the labourers were being repressed by military force, the terror of fires had produced attention, and the beginnings of change: 'Without entering at present into the *motives* of the working people, it is unquestionable that their acts have produced good, and great good too' (11.12.1830). It was for this dangerously honest recognition that Cobbett was again prosecuted. His trial in July 1831 took place within the continued reform agitation; the jury split, and the prosecution was dropped. A limited

Reform Bill passed the Commons in September but was rejected
by the Lords. In October and November there were serious riots
in Derby, Nottingham and Bristol. In December a new Bill went
through the Commons; in June 1832, after many delaying ma-
noeuvres, it passed the Lords. An effective interaction of argument and revolt was again evident.

Cobbett, now sixty-nine, went on travelling and campaigning
for greater reforms: for manhood suffrage, the ballot and
annual election. In the new general election he was returned for
Oldham. He spent his last years as an uneasy Member of Parliament. When the Houses of Parliament burned down, in 1834, he
could not 'refrain from offering a remark or two':

> My insipid friend says, 'that the MOB' (meaning the people of
> London), 'when they *saw the progress of the flames*, raised a
> SAVAGE shout of EXULTATION'. Did they indeed? The
> *Herald* exclaims, 'O, UNREFLECTING people!' Now perhaps
> the 'MOB' exulted because the 'MOB' was really a *reflecting*
> 'mob'. When even a dog, or a horse, receives any treatment
> that it does not like, it always *shuns the place* where it got
> such treatment ... (1.11.1834)

And he went on to list the acts of repression and omission which
had occurred 'in this same HOUSE'. 'Oh! God of mercy!'

1835

Cobbett continued to campaign, over a wide range of causes:
for a reduction of the working day to ten hours (it settled at
twelve); against the new Poor Law and its workhouses; for relief
and political change in Ireland, which he toured. In his marriage
and family life, his last years were unhappy, with estrangement
from at latest 1827 and an effective break from 1833. After
1833, also, he was often ill and had great difficulty in sleeping.
After several late sittings of the House of Commons in May
1835, he became very ill with renewed inflammation of the
throat. On Wednesday 3 June he was carried around his farm.
In the early hours of Thursday 4 June he died.

2 Themes

Cobbett wrote over a period of forty years, and in their course not only several of his opinions but some of his most basic affiliations changed. Moreover, though he wrote extensively and persistently on certain matters, and very thoroughly on some, he cannot be said to have produced any connected and systematic set of ideas, though he undoubtedly achieved, in his mature work, a coherent and powerful body of positions. To analyse his work, then, is not to articulate a system but to consider certain dominant themes.

In the present chapter, three of these will be discussed: poverty, labour and property; liberty and democracy; education and the Press. A fourth and broader theme – the rural economy in its relations both to a developing industrialism and to the capitalist system and state – will be more extensively discussed in the third chapter.

Poverty, labour and property

The question of poverty can be seen as the centre of all Cobbett's work. Certainly it is the living issue to which, in the end, he refers all other questions. How then does he see poverty?

> By poverty, I mean real want, a real insufficiency of the food and raiment and lodging necessary to health and decency; and not that imaginary poverty, of which some persons complain. The man who, by his own and his family's labour, can provide a sufficiency of food and raiment, and a comfortable dwelling-place, is not a poor man. There must be different ranks and degrees in every civil society, and, indeed, so it is even amongst the savage tribes. There must be different degrees of wealth; some must have more than others; and the richest must be a great deal richer than the least rich. But it is necessary to the very existence of a people, that nine out of

ten should live wholly by the sweat of their brow; and, is it not degrading to human nature, that all the nine-tenths should be called poor; and, what is still worse, call themselves poor, and be contented in that degraded state? (C 3)

The reference is to what is now called 'absolute poverty'. Cobbett is not addressing himself to the questions involved in the important modern definition of 'relative poverty', from which, as a society develops, new standards of need are generalised, and what are wants and deficiencies by these new and changing standards are reasonably seen as 'deprivation' and hence poverty. Cobbett's is, in this context, a more limited idea; yet not only in the England of his day, but in the world of our own day, in which at least *eight hundred million* people live in such absolute poverty, it is a profound and in its application radical idea.

Cobbett applied the idea in two main ways: historical and political. The historical application had two points of reference. First, and persistent, was the comparison of the first decades of the nineteenth century with those of his own boyhood: 'You may cry Jacobin and Leveller as long as you please. I wish to see the poor men of England what the poor men of England were when I was born' (28.2.1807). Again:

There are hundreds of thousands of the people of England who never taste any food but bread and vegetables, and who scarcely even know what it is to have a full meal even of these. This is *new*: it was not so in former times: it was not so even till of *late* years. (8.2.1806)

In his later writing, while retaining this point of view, Cobbett put forward a broader historical argument: that the Protestant Reformation was the origin of the system of funding and taxing, corruption and privilege, which had pauperism as its most damaging consequence.

There are historical problems with both these arguments. The problem of the new financial State will be considered below. In the comparison with the 1760s and 1770s, Cobbett speaks, evidently, with some direct authority, but, first, he is comparing his own then relatively prosperous district, in a period of relative stability, with many districts in a period of dislocation by a war and its consequences; and, second, he is comparing one part of an older rural economy with many parts of a rural economy radically changed by the full effects of enclosures, increasing population and a new poor-relief system. It is extremely difficult, through the intricacies of comparisons within varying districts and changing economic and social conditions, either to confirm or to reject Cobbett's central assertion. What mattered at the time, and especially at the worst times – the years around 1806, 1816, 1822 and 1830 – was that Cobbett was expressing a widespread popular conviction.

This is the basis of the political application. Cobbett is asserting, as a principle, that labour shall not produce poverty. He is also observing that under the prevailing system this is indeed what it produces:

A very large portion of the agricultural labourers of England: a very large portion of those who raise all the food, who make all the buildings, who prepare all the fuel, who, in short, by their labour sustain the community; a very large part of these exist in a state of almost incessant hunger. (30.8.1823)

These were the producers of food, buildings, fuel. As for the producers of clothing:

The great towns, and particularly the manufacturing districts, are daily increasing in numbers … These masses are still more miserable than the wretches left behind them in the agricultural districts … In the cotton-spinning work, these creatures are kept, fourteen hours in each day, locked up, summer and winter, in a heat of from EIGHTY TO EIGHTYFOUR DEGREES … three hundred and thirteen days in the year … Well constitutioned men are rendered old and past labour at forty years of age, and … children are rendered decrepit and deformed, and thousands upon thousands of them slaughtered by consumptions. (20.11.1824)

Even their very low wages are largely clawed back by manipulated food-prices and rents.

Thus the natural relation between labour and sufficiency has been destroyed, and an unnatural relation between labour and poverty established. Accordingly the unnatural relation must be destroyed, and the natural relation restored. This is at the centre of all Cobbett's political arguments:

> To live well, to enjoy all things that make life pleasant, is the right of every man who constantly uses his strength judiciously and lawfully. It is to blaspheme God to suppose that he created men to be miserable, to hunger, thirst, and perish with cold, in the midst of that abundance which is the fruit of their own labour. Instead, therefore, of applauding 'happy poverty', which applause is so much the fashion of the present day, I despise the man that is poor and contented; for such content is a certain proof of a base disposition, a disposition which is the enemy of all industry, all exertion, all love of independence. (C 2–3)

This position overlaps with many other arguments about labour and poverty which have since separated out and even come into opposition with each other. Thus there is a strong emphasis on the need and even duty to work hard, and this is related to personal character. A version of this position, detached from the other parts of Cobbett's argument, came through later as the Self-Help recommendation, and is still heard, as a response to arguments about poverty and unemployment, in our own time.

Yet Cobbett's stress on effort and character is inseparable from his argument that the relation between these and a sufficiency has been systematically distorted. Moreover, it is from Cobbett's contempt for the man who is 'poor and contented' that his whole politics proceeds. It was upon this principle that he based his support for or sympathy with all the means of redress: not only political reform but, in the absence of adequate political action, strikes, riots and arson. He always preferred and recommended the most peaceable ways, but the strength of his position in the most critical years is that the argument from character — an honest and hard-working man should strive to change his own condition — is extended to a class and a people: that if they respect themselves they *must* act by any efficient means to change their collective conditions.

The false quantity in the orthodox equation between hard work and a sufficiency is, of course, the prior existence of property and its advantages and privileges. Cobbett believed very strongly in the rights of property, and said many things which, on their own, can be appropriated by those who would make the defence of property the first principle of politics. Yet he believed so strongly in property that he carried the argument to a wholly radical plane.

Thus, first, on the right of working people to combine (then forbidden by law) and to withdraw their labour:

> The principle upon which all property exists is this: that a man has a right to do with it that which he pleases. That he has a right to sell it, or to keep it. That he has a right to refuse to part with it at all: or, if he choose to sell it, to insist upon any price that he chooses to demand: if this be not the case, a man has no property ... When it was found that men could not keep their families decently upon the wages that the rich masters chose to give them, and that the men would *not work*, and contrived to combine ... it was found necessary so to *torture the laws* as to punish men for demanding what they deemed the worth of their labour. (19.12.1818)

It is the very familiarity of the conventional first stages of the argument which produces the shock (certainly then; in some places still) of the application of the principle to people for whom it was clearly not intended: the rights of the propertyless in their only property, labour.

But Cobbett also went significantly deeper into the nature of property itself:

> The land, the trees, the fruits, the herbage, the roots are, by the law of nature, the common possession of all the people. The social compact, entered into for their mutual *benefit* and *protection* ... gives rise, at once, to the words *mine* and *thine*. Men exert their skill and strength upon particular spots of land. These become *their own*. And, when laws come to be made, these spots are called the *property* of the owners. But

still the property, in land especially, can never be so *complete* and *absolute* as to give to the proprietors the right of with-holding the means of existence, or of animal enjoyment, from any portion of the people; seeing that the very foundation of the compact was, the *protection* and *benefit* of the whole ... And, if a contingency arise, in which men ... are unable, by moderate labour ... to obtain food sufficient for themselves and their women and children, there is no longer *benefit* and *protection* to the whole; the social compact is at an end; and men have a right, thenceforward, to act agreeably to the laws of nature. (8.5.1819)

Again the argument is cast in conventional terms: the abstrac-tion of a social contract rather than the historical character of class society. Yet it is by taking the convention fully and seriously, beyond its practically biased applications, that Cobbett arrives at a subversive dissolution of the property rights of the existing state. A position already well known in theories of natural law, on the ultimate human right to means of subsist-ence, is sharply asserted and applied within an actual crisis to which its terms are immediately relevant, and is related to an actual social structure of property and class. It is not surprising that he goes on to argue against the extension from Ireland to England of a '*police-force*' to defend the existing proprietors against the people exercising their natural rights: a '*force*', moreover, to be 'paid for by the industrious people' (6.4.1833).

Cobbett was far from alone, in this period, in arguing for the rights of labour and against the existing system of property. It was the period of the beginnings of the modern labour move-ment and of the early arguments for socialism. In almost all his arguments about labour and property, Cobbett mainly applies the ideas and the arguments of the social order within which he supposed himself to be living, to the actual social order in two of its inescapable aspects: a major crisis of employment and sub-sistence, which was daily controverting its supposed principles and laws; and a crisis of legitimacy in which, behind the screen of these laws and principles, actual and widespread corruption and repression were the practical standards by which society was governed. The shock of the outraged believer in the supposed principles of bourgeois society was in itself a major radicalism. What made it widely effective was an extension of the supposed principles: an extension to all men, rather than just the proprietors and entrepreneurs by and for whom the principles had been devised.

This is indeed the inner history of the radicalism of the period, most notably in the cases of parliamentary reform and the new Poor Law. One major radical tendency was in effect fulfilled by this legislation, and a century of its kind of reforms followed. Cobbett, at the very edge of his thinking, was moving beyond these kinds of change. What counted was his practical affiliation to the great majority of working and poor people, whose rights and needs went far beyond the perspective of such limited reforms.

This division of tendencies was present throughout the period, but it only became quite open and acute in the 1830s, in the very last years of Cobbett's life. Thus though in practice he was prefiguring the later movement – in his unbreakable attachment to the popular majority of the working people, and in his refusal to be intimidated by a class-based law or by the customary social and cultural constraints – he did not in fact reach its characteristic shaping ideas.

Thus, in his implacable opposition to extensive public taxation and new statutory provisions, he was an enemy not only of the limited reformers but of a major tendency in the development of the labour movement. He supported laws to protect the conditions of labour, as in the campaigns for shorter hours and for holidays. He was always also an advocate of better wages. His real problem came in considering those who were, for whatever reason, unable to work. He was a vigorous supporter of the old Poor Law, which he interpreted as giving a right to relief in the basic fact of common property, immediately chargeable on existing property-holders. He then fiercely opposed its interpretation or modification as 'charity', which he called the 'comforting system':

The tendency of the funding and taxing system is, carried to its extreme, to draw the produce of the labour into unnatural channels, into the hands of upstart cormorants, and to deal it back again in driblets, under the name of relief or of charity, just to support the life of those from whose pores it has been drained. (8.2.1806)

This radical position, within the actual taxing system of his day, set him against those tendencies which would culminate in the 'Welfare State'. Indeed as a critique of some aspects of the Welfare State under capitalism it remains valid. He was bitterly hostile to the new Poor Law, centrally administered and trying to deal with new forms of poverty, but based on the cruel premise that poverty was a personal fault or crime, to be treated in such ways as to drive people to work under any conditions. This driving element has never been entirely removed, even from 'welfare' legislation, although in general the premise has been revised.

Yet, deriving the right of relief from an older kind of economy, or from its idealisation, Cobbett halted, deliberately, at the threshold of new kinds of co-operative and collective social provision. The rights of the labourers and of the poor belonged in the old 'moral economy', based on ideas of a supposedly permanent interdependence, and he was impatient not only with cruel and indifferent attempts to destroy this but with the first phases of conception of and struggle for some new 'moral economy' (Paine, for example, and then Owen and others, saw more of this possibility).

The case is just as clear in the matter of *class* organisation, which was to prove so decisive. Cobbett was much too close to the realities of his time to deny the existence of social classes, and he gave extraordinary energy to demonstrating the facts of class exploitation, as between proprietors and *rentiers* on the one hand, and artisans and labourers on the other. Yet what he saw, correctly, as the increasing polarisation of these classes was for him just one more symptom of the crisis caused by the financial system:

Amongst these effects are the present *combinations of the*

working classes ... They combine to effect a rise in wages. The masters combine against them. One side complains of the other; but, neither knows the *cause* of the turmoil, and the turmoil goes on. The different trades combine, and call their combination a GENERAL UNION. So that here is one class of society united to oppose another class. (27.8.1825).

The fact is recognised, understood, but regretted. It was primarily the actions of the ruling class, through its dishonourable and corrupt financial system, which were producing this profound social division and conflict. Yet it is significant that it was in an argument directed to the Nottingham stocking-weavers that he made one of his clearest attacks on class polarisation. It had been said that the weavers' low wages were the result of unfair competition by 'bagmen', who snatched 'the bread from the mouth of the workmen, and the fair profits from the hands of the regular and honourable manufacturers'. This would be a characteristic instance of working-class pressure to maintain and regulate the established conditions of trade, for their own protection. Cobbett was indignant:

> You are for an *aristocracy* in trade: you are for Lords of the Loom: you are for shutting out your own brother workmen, your own kindred and children ... You are for cutting off the chain of connection between the rich and the poor. You are for demolishing all small tradesmen. You are for reducing the community to two classes: *Masters* and *Slaves*. (14.4.1821)

The underlying argument, evidently, is for social mobility. Cobbett regularly instanced himself as a man who had risen in the world by his own efforts. He was against any forces or arguments which hindered what he saw as this natural mobility. The principal destroyer of this mobility, and of the consequent diversity of the community, was the financial system which had 'drawn the real property of the nation into fewer hands' (6.12.1806); 'the resources of the country ... drawn unnaturally together into great heaps' (8.3.1834). The evil result was that 'we are daily advancing to the state in which there are but two classes of men, *masters*, and *abject dependants*' (6.12.1806). His model was an older, more extended and diverse system: 'When *master* and *man* were the terms, every one was in his place; and all were free. Now, in fact, it is an affair of *masters* and *slaves*' (14.4.1821). Thus, as we should now say, the concentration of capital and of ownership of the means of production was destroying the diversity and with it the natural mobility of the community. The new capitalists were mocked as a version of the hated landed aristocracy: 'Seigneurs of the Twist, sovereigns of the Spinning Jenny, great Yeomen of the Yarn' (10.7.1824). Systematic and inhuman relations were being established, in 'the new-fangled jargon of *Employer* and *Operative*'.

There is never any doubt of Cobbett's hatred of the great proprietors and manufacturers, but one of the reasons for hating them, second only to their cruelty in the imposition of poverty on their labourers, is that, as they concentrate and organise, they are creating the modern class system. Within this perspective, he understands and supports the defensive organisations of workers, but if he sees them settling for and thinking inside this new fixed system, even as class against class, he sees them as wrong. This is one of several instances when Cobbett's older kind of radicalism – based, as is obvious, not only on an old and idealised social model, but also on a limited understanding of the new forces and relations of industrial production – is at once limited and partial in his own day yet, in broader terms, still relevant and even prophetic.

Liberty and democracy

The *words* rights, liberty, freedom, and the like, the *mere words*, are not worth a straw; and very frequently they serve as a cheat. What is the sound of liberty to a man who is compelled to work constantly and who is still, in spite of his toil, his vigilance, his frugality, half naked and half starved! In such a case the word liberty is abused: such a man is a slave, whatever he may call himself. (T 5.1.1831)

Cobbett's central idea of freedom is always material, even physical. This is the firm ground of his political sanity. It is what changed him from an anti-democratic pamphleteer in the 1790s

to the radical campaigner of all his later years. For it is possible
to throw around or even, more rationally, to exchange political
ideas, within a limited social circle, and still to be talking about
almost everything but the real conditions of human life. Cobbett
was all for Law and Order, and for the Traditions of his
Country, until he saw people starving or half-starving in the
shadow of such ideas. The hard cutting-edge of his mind got
through to a primarily material politics. Whatever else it might
later be necessary to consider, the physical means of sustaining
and reproducing life were always where the argument must start
and what it must be judged by.

Thus it was at a second stage that he joined the more familiar
arguments about liberty and democracy. Many of his arguments
about liberty always remained functional. Indeed most of his
emphasis was on the right of honest men to expose and name
scoundrels. He argued this as vigorously when he was in fact
denouncing honest men, Priestley and Paine and Rush, as when
he was pursuing the evidently corrupt or the nominally respectable tax-eaters and sinecurists. Yet the habit grew into a principle, within the real conditions of his time:

> It is farcical to talk about freedom of the press, unless by it we
> mean the *right*, the acknowledged *legal right*, of freely
> expressing our opinions, be they what they may, *respecting
> the character and conduct of men in power*; and of stating
> anything, no matter what, if we can prove the *truth* of the
> statement. (4.2.1809)

This was a conscious and necessary challenge to a system of law
which made it an offence, in England, to 'bring into hatred or
contempt', or even to create dissatisfaction with, the King, the
Government and the Law Courts themselves. Moreover this was
not a sleeping statute. It was the ground on which Cobbett was
gaoled for his protest about the flogging of English militiamen
under the guard of foreign mercenaries.

An instrumental liberty thus became a general cause. At the
time of the *History of the Last Hundred Days of English
Freedom*, in 1817, Cobbett was able to trace a whole system of

gagging, repression and government spies. He was right about the system, but his title reveals his perspective. There had been freedom in England until the present gang of rulers came along to destroy it. As he put it to the journeymen and labourers:

> There is no principle, no precedent, no regulations (except as to mere matter of detail), favourable to freedom, which is not to be found in the Laws of England or in the example of our Ancestors. Therefore, I say we may ask for, and we want *nothing new*. We have great constitutional laws and principles, to which we are unmoveably attached. We want *great alteration*, but we want *nothing new*. (2.11.1816)

This was not only Cobbett's view. It was widely shared by many of the most radical reformers, though they differed as to the period in which this essential and virtually timeless English freedom had been suppressed: by the Normans; by the centralising State which emerged after the 'Glorious Revolution' of 1688; by the new, centrally appointed magistracy; by the borough-mongers and tax-eaters; by the gagging Ministry of the Hundred Days. There was thus the strange case, not without its effects on later myths and practices of English politics, of people fighting a tyrannical and repressive system and demanding, as Cobbett insisted, not just an '*efficient*' but a '*radical* Reform' (1.6.1822), who at the same time declared and believed that they were essentially engaged in a *restoration*: that they wanted 'nothing new'.

Cobbett's hold on the material character of freedom is here at its loosest. He began by wanting to end corruption, which was the source of exploitation and fraud in all their forms. His earliest complaints about the actual Parliament of England were that it was filled with placemen and pensioners and sinecurists, and that votes were openly bought. If only honest men would refuse to bribe and be bribed, and other honest men would elect them, all evils of the system would be remedied. Thus: 'I have had too much opportunity of studying men and things to be led astray by any *wild theories about liberty* ... All I wish and all I strive for is *The Constitution of England*, undefiled by corruption' (15.4.1809).

This idealising separation, between the Constitution and the system of exploitation and fraud which was so notably flourishing 'under' or 'beside' it, could not be sustained in the hard practice of those years, though to an extraordinary extent it went on being sustained as an idea. Cobbett moved on from the isolation of bribery to the organisation of 'representation', which was systematically corrupt. By 1816 he was supporting a reform of Parliament by extending the vote to all direct taxpayers, at the same time deliberately excluding all others. This was to be a reform of the House of Commons only. The House of Lords and the monarchy, whatever might be said of them on other grounds, were to remain as they were. This follows from the attachment to 'The Constitution', and is of course directly related to the orthodox equation of the right of government with the possession of property. Within this as yet unquestioned equation, both the material freedoms of the inarticulate majority (their right to the necessities of life) and the political freedoms of the articulate minority would be secured. Direct action to remedy distress or to end exploitation can be sympathetically understood but must be firmly discouraged. The parliamentary reform would see to all that.

The years and the arguments moved on. By the 1820s, and particularly the late 1820s, Cobbett had changed the means, though he stayed with the remedy:

> It is hard to say what, amongst all the contrivances that will be hatched for the purpose of giving the name and withholding the substance of reform; amongst all the schemes that will be tried to cajole and deceive the people ... it is hardly possible to guess at what precise point of shadow, shutting out the substance, the projectors will rest; but, let us suppose, that, alarmed at present appearances; let us suppose that, bearing in mind the deeds of the working people of Paris and of Brussels, and estimating the effect of those deeds upon the minds of the mass of the people in England; let us suppose that, at last, and at the eleventh hour, it be resolved to do

something; and let us even suppose that it be in the midst of daily-increasing dangers resolved to abolish the infernal boroughs of every description and to give the people their fair choice, only confining the right of voting to householders . . . Let us suppose that they are, at last, willing to give a vote to every man that occupies a house, whether he pay direct taxes or not. Then, this does not satisfy me. It ought not to satisfy you, and it will not give peace and happiness and freedom to the country. (30.10.1830)

This is Cobbett's mature position. It corresponds with his clear affiliation to the majority of working men. It is affected by his recognition of the justice of the labourers' revolt. It is part of a much broader and more general political perspective, as in his welcome to the French and Belgian revolutions ('the deeds of the working people of Paris and of Brussels'). 'All Europe is in a state of commotion, every-where are the people on foot to obtain a just share in the government of their country; and is it to be believed that England is the only country in which the people are not to succeed!' (26.3.1831). Again, more firmly, on the events in France: 'I am pleased at the Revolution, particularly on this account, that it makes the working classes see their real importance, and those who despise them see it too' (F 1).

What has effectively happened, by this stage, is a shift from an idea of constitutional reform to an idea of democracy. It should be remembered, as we look back, how radical an idea democracy then was (Cobbett's abuse of it in the 1790s is characteristic). Today, in Western Europe and North America, almost everyone offers to believe in it; only a few candid reactionaries oppose it by name. Yet the division that was open in England, around 1832, between constitutional reform and active democracy remains crucial. Cobbett's shift is twofold. He now wants to break the equation between property and voting rights: the deep principle on which the supposed free constitution had been founded. In slow and grudging reforms, dragged out under pressure over the subsequent hundred years, this was at last in general achieved. But there is another and more radical shift. The direct exertion of popular pressure is now openly welcomed. This is so whether it is to hurry on parliamentary reform or, as in the case of the labourers' revolt, to improve their immediate conditions. It was just such direct action, open popular intervention in the politics and economics of the country, that was then generally seen as democracy, and by the ruling and privileged class as the 'democratic threat'. A material freedom was becoming practical and active.

At the same time Cobbett still believed that the immediate way forward was parliamentary reform. In 1830, in line with other radicals, he put forward his short programme: annually elected parliaments; one man one vote (from the age of eighteen); three years' residence as a qualification for parliamentary candidacy in a constituency; secret ballot. A century and a half later, two of these items have been enacted. One woman one vote, with which Cobbett and almost all others of his time would have nothing to do, has also been enacted. A necessary argument about parliamentary and constitutional reform is still active.

Yet we have to look beyond this immediate detail to more general questions. Cobbett was quite sure that a properly reformed parliament would put an end to the poverty and oppression of the working people. 'The enemies of reform jeeringly ask us, whether reform would do these things for us; and I answer distinctly that IT WOULD DO THEM ALL!' (2.4.1831). The certainty of this conviction, against the enemies of reform, is in one way admirable. Cobbett had shown clearly enough, from his starting-point in the material freedom and material needs of the working people, that this is what he wanted reform for. He lived only three years after the limited 1832 reform of Parliament, and saw none of these things happen. Indeed he saw and had to fight the cruelties of a new Poor Law. Obviously he still believed that more radical reforms of voting and representation were necessary.

But there is another element in his perception of the evils of the unreformed parliamentary system:

The words Tory and Whig now excite ridicule and contempt at the bare sound of them. The words '*opposition*' and '*gentlemen opposite*' are becoming equally contemptible. The people have long looked upon the whole as one mass of fellows fighting and scrambling for public money; some fighting to keep it, and others scrambling to get at it; some dogs in possession of the carcase, and some growling and barking because they cannot get a share. Seeing the people despising both these factions, a *third* has started, to whom I have always given the name of SHOY-HOYS; and now I will tell you why. (T 1.9.1830)

This is the old angry Cobbett, extending his lifelong attack on corruption and sinecurism to the party system. He was as hard about this after the reforms as before. But before 1832 there were also the 'shoy-hoys', scarecrows:

The people want a reform of the parliament, and there has for a long time ... been a little band, who have professed a desire to get parliamentary reform. They have made motions and speeches and divisions, with a view of keeping the hopes of the people alive, and have thereby been able to keep them quiet from time to time. They have never desired to *succeed*; because success would put an end to their hopes of emolument; but they have amused the people. The great body of the factions, knowing the reality of their views, have been highly diverted by their sham efforts, which have never interrupted them in the smallest degree in their enjoyment of the general plunder. Just as it happens with the birds and the shoy-hoys in the fields or gardens. At first, the birds take the shoy-hoy for a *real* man or woman; and, so long as they do this, they abstain from their work of plunder; but after having for some little while watched the shoy-hoy with their quick and piercing eyes, and perceived that it never moves hand or foot, they totally disregard it, and are no more obstructed by it than if it were a post.

Those particular shoy-hoys were on pre-1832 ground. But it is difficult to read Cobbett's description of them without thinking of many others of the same type. The question goes to the root of the hopes which Cobbett and others pinned on parliamentary reform. After 1832 Cobbett wondered whether aristocratic privilege, the 'Old Corruption', had not simply been replaced by the rule of the 'money-men'. In those last, failing years he sought for other local remedies: he was against the cabinet system and the party system; he considered a more direct relation between the monarchy and a parliament by universal suffrage, including now a partly reformed House of Lords. Yet these positions were little to the point. What was really being tested, in those and in all the succeeding years, was the assumed relation between a representative electoral system and the real processes of the economy and society. Cobbett, starting where he did, with a material definition of freedom and rights, at once assumed this relation as directive – a reformed Parliament would end poverty – and yet continually broke through to the harder realisation that there was a whole wide system of 'plunder' – of systematic exploitation – and that it would need quite extraordinary effort to end this: effort which could be distantly interpreted as constitutional reform but which had continually to push past both the factions and the shoy-hoys if it was to succeed where it mattered: in the daily lives of the working people.

Education and the Press

Many of Cobbett's ideas jump at us from his pages. It is as if we can hear him speaking them, in his usual plain and simple and decided way. His particular ideas on education share this quality, but we have only to try to put them together, as general ideas, to discover something more complex, and something which is often, partly through his fault, misunderstood.

It is necessary to look first at what he thought of traditional education, as it had come down from the Renaissance grammar schools to the privileged education of the modern period. He went straight to the class character of this education, which was centred in its definition of the 'learned languages':

If this be the meaning of the '*Uti Possidetis*', why not give us that meaning in our own language at once? Do those who make use of such phrases, which the stupidest wretch upon earth might learn to use as well as they, in a few hours; nay, which a parrot would learn, or which a high-dutch bird-catcher would teach to a bull-finch or a tom-tit, in the space of a month; and do they think, in good earnest, that this relick of the mummery of monkery, this playing off upon us of a few gallipot words, will make us believe that they are *learned*? Learning, truly so called, consists in the possession of knowledge and in the capacity of communicating that knowledge to others; and, as far as my observation will enable me to speak, what are called the *learned* languages, operate as a bar to the acquirement of real learning. (10.1.1807)

The schools and colleges which define education in terms of these languages are conscious elements of an exploiting system: 'The Aristocracy have a deep interest in the upholding of this *learned* system of cheat and oppression' (29.11.1817). This is so in the organised connections of such places with landed property and benefices, and in their internal organisation, including the 'poor scholars': 'here the needy learn in their youth to crawl to the rich and powerful'. It is even more so in the kind of mind that such schools and colleges form:

It is no small mischief to a boy, that many of the best years of his life should be devoted to the learning of what can never be of any real use to any human being. His mind is necessarily rendered frivolous and superficial by the long habit of attaching importance to *words* instead of *things*; to *sound* instead of *sense* ... Is it not fortunate if half a life restore the energies of mind thus enfeebled at the outset? Must it not be a sort of miracle, if a bold thought, an original idea, ever come from such a mind? ... However, the general effect is, to accustom the mind, by slow degrees, to those trammels, in which, at last, it is not only content to remain, but for which it acquires a taste, at the same time, that it acquires a conceit, that superiority consists chiefly in the having been at a college. Hence this race of men are, at once, the most ignorant and the most conceited in the world; and, if they are of the *dependent* class, they have all the pride of the noble with far more than all the meanness of his meanest domestic servant. When you meet with one of them at a time, he wearies you half to death with his *puns*, his college jokes, and scraps; but, if two, they are a perfect pest. A loud tone and pulpit-like gesticulations they have learnt to great perfection, and ill-manners are the natural produce of their insolent conceit and fancied superiority. In a company, however numerous, they soon smell each other out. One or the other soon finds occasion, or makes occasion, to let it be known, that he has been at *Oxford* or *Cambridge* . . .

It is remarkable to think that this was written more than a century and a half ago, across so many great changes. The extraordinary persistence of this at once intellectual and social formation, in those who still define themselves in class terms as 'the educated', is a central factor of British history. Contemporary arguments against the fee-paying schools are most frequently cast in terms of their social privileges, which are indeed still real. But the central argument against them, in Cobbett's time as in our own, is *intellectual*: is against the *kind of mind*, the mental habits and signals, which they indeed so efficiently reproduce.

One of these signals is that such criticism is the 'envy' of the 'autodidact' (the prevailing name for those, however learned or intellectually capable, who were educated within some other system). Cobbett knew this taunt, and issued his challenges to public argument. The signals clicked on. Cobbett stuck to his general argument: 'Here, in short, is everything to render the great full of insolent pride, and the poor subservient and base' (29.11.1817).

It is necessary to observe the close association asserted by Cobbett between the form and content of education and its actual (open or hidden) social functions if we are to understand his opinions on *popular* education. Thus we might quote: 'I am wholly against children wasting their time in the idleness of what is called education' (C 7). But it is necessary to complete the quotation: 'and particularly in schools over which the parents have no control, and where nothing is taught but the rudiments of servility, pauperism, and slavery.' That 'nothing' is of course an exaggeration, but Cobbett, even at his most prejudiced, was right to refuse to abstract formal instruction from the teaching and practice of social relationships which almost inevitably accompany and influence it. Education, he insisted, was this whole process of formation, and the first question to ask was: Who is in control of it? Thus he attacked the new Society for the Diffusion of Useful Knowledge: 'This, like all the rest of the '*education*' schemes, is a combination for the purpose of *amusing* the working classes, and *diverting their attention from the cause of their poverty and misery*' (29.5.1830). He was cautious about the new Mechanics' Institutes:

> I gave my five pounds as a mark of my regard for and my attachment to the *working classes of the community*, and also as a mark of my approbation of any thing which seemed to assert that these classes were equal, in point of intellect, to those who have had the insolence to call them the '*Lower Orders*'. But, I was not without my fears, that this institution may be turned to purposes, *extremely injurious to the mechanics* themselves. I cannot but know what sort of people are likely to get amongst them ... Mechanics, I most heartily *wish you well*; but I also most heartily wish you not to be *humbugged*, which you most certainly will be, if you suffer any body but REAL MECHANICS to have anything to do in managing the concern. You will *mean well*; but, many a cunning scoundrel will get *place* or *pension* as the *price* of you ... (15.11.1823)

He was openly hostile to the new schools and classes under religious patronage:

> Education means, not the reading of books; not the being able to read and sing the psalms of Sternhold and Hopkins ... it means *breeding-up*, and ... people may be brought up very well, and especially to the most numerous sorts of *work*, without any reading at all. But, taking education to mean reading and writing; or, in other words, knowledge to be got from books; what knowledge, I pray you, are the people to get from those '*religious tracts*' ...? (5.2.1825)

He was against these tracts because they taught submission to a natural order or a higher will, and thus concealed the real causes of poverty and weakened the impulse to remove them. He was just as much against the calculating view of education for social advantage within the existing relations of exploitation: 'The taste of the times is, unhappily, to give to children something of book-learning, with a view of placing them to live, in some way or other, upon the labour of other people' (C 6).

Yet while he was getting through to the real content of so many educational institutions and projects, not only as they appeared in his own time but as they were subsequently established and extended, his own mind was blocked in two important ways. First, he largely missed the contradictory effect of the various schemes to teach working people and their children to read. He tended to see only the tracts and 'comforting' which were among the most immediate reading material. But in fact there was no way in which poor people could be taught to read such matter which did not also enable them to read . . . Cobbett! Very many poor men who were his actual readers had learned to read under the very patronage which he attacked. He was justly conscious that he was a *competitor* for such readers; the vanity of manner with which he often asserted this does not alter the fact that there was this crucial struggle of ideas, through the means of literacy and print.

The second block in his mind was also a matter of contradiction, within the real complexities of the whole social process. He believed that the existing social system exploited the working people. He also believed that there was a 'natural' form of social mobility which could get beyond this: his own life was his leading case. But then, contradicting his own example, he asserted that this 'natural progress' (C 7) must be gradual, and therefore that the general education of labourers would lead only to disappointment and misery, spoiling them as labourers and leading them into conceit and desperation. With his mind still held by a static model of society, in which even radical reform would do no more than restore a properly ordered system based on a necessary division of labour, Cobbett moved by the very force of his indignation to an evidently reactionary position, in which education is to be graded to actual or inevitable social class, and the labourers taught first the skills of bodily labour and only then, 'if the ability remain', 'book-learning'. This is an absurdly contradictory position in relation to Cobbett's own practice. He addressed his *Advice to Young Men*, with many details about formal education, to those 'in the Middle and Higher Ranks of Life'. But he addressed *Cottage Economy* to 'the Labouring Classes of this Kingdom', making its content the skills of maintaining practical life, yet embodying this content *in print*.

This becomes a quite central contradiction. The separation of education from work and practice, which he had attacked in its influential embodiment in the grammar-school curriculum, was not likely to be ended by turning the same separation upside-down: offering the working people labouring skills and honest wages but not literacy and learning. What Cobbett had in fact seized on, as the main weapon against the force and fraud by which the exploiting system was maintained, was a particular form of public education: not only his campaigning journalism, which required general literacy, but also his long series of books of instruction, in grammar and history. Thus he failed, theoretically, to confirm his own real practice.

Yet what remains, within this failure, on the purpose and content of education, is still significant. Few advocates of popular education, from his day to ours, have seen so clearly that it is never only a matter of subjects but is always also a process of social formation. His anger and impatience at the schemes of his day reach across the long years to several contemporary positions about education and class relations, education and ideology. On the content of teaching, he has certain obvious prejudices, notably against most literature and art, but at the same time proposes a common curriculum (within the class restrictions already noted) which is better than most of those of his time. His core is 'grammar, arithmetic, history ... geography'. His most useful argument is on history:

The histories of England ... are very little better than

romances. Their contents are generally confined to narrations relating to battles, negotiations, intrigues, contests between rival sovereignties, rival nobles, and to the character of kings, queens, mistresses, bishops, ministers and the like ... I remember, that, about a dozen years ago, I was talking with a very clever young man, who had read twice or thrice over the History of England, by different authors; and that I gave the conversation a turn that drew from him, unperceived by himself, that he did not know how tithes, parishes, poor-rates, church-rates, and the abolition of trial by jury in hundreds of cases, came to be in England ... We do not want to consume our time over a dozen pages about Edward the Third dancing at a ball, picking up a lady's garter, and making that garter the foundation of an order of knighthood, bearing the motto of 'Honi soit qui mal y pense'. It is not stuff like this; but we want to know what was the state of the people; what were a labourer's wages; what were the prices of the food, and how the labourers were dressed in the reign of that great king. (A 301–3)

If it is true (as most now agree) that Cobbett's own historical writing, especially on the effects of the Reformation, is riddled with errors in just this general area, we can refer the fault not only to him but to the kind of history – in fact still widely taught and propagated – which brought detailed research to bear on the 'stuff' and left most people, including scholars, ignorant or deluded about the substance.

Of course Cobbett's real drive, in the case of history as in everything else, was to change conditions in his own place and time. He published books and pamphlets, but his central effort was in the Press, in journalism. We have seen how much of his general argument for liberty was in terms of the liberty of the Press. We can now look at his idea of the purposes and contents of journalism, since this is in close relation with his leading ideas in education.

When he started the *Register*, which under different forms and titles was to run for thirty-three years, he listed its proposed contents. These included abridged proceedings of Parliament;

all State papers; and four categories (promotions of peers, statesmen and officers; births, deaths and marriages of nobility and Parliament; financial news; corn and bread prices) which he described 'not as subject of tittle-tattle, but as facts connected with history and political economy' (16.1.1802). He also proposed to refuse advertisements, 'the great source of emolument', and observed that 'some papers ... are the property of companies of traders or speculators. The thing is regarded merely as a money speculation ... and, of course, the most profitable politics will be always preferred' (11.4.1807). He was thus setting himself, not only against the repressive laws which restricted or crushed the freedom of the Press (laws which were at their most severe during his working life), but against the wider organisation of the Press as a commercial system, linked with the ruling class, which in fact outlasted the repressive laws and came through as dominant; indeed as our modern 'free Press'.

Cobbett was in general right about the newspapers he opposed. His most famous attack, at the time of the labourers' revolt in 1830, still has bite:

> Will this Ministry *shed their blood*? ... The bloody old *Times* newspaper, which is the organ, and, perhaps, in great part the *property*, of this hellish crew, says, that the labourers '*are starving*, and that they have been *cruelly oppressed*; but that *some* of them must be made to suffer the *severest penalty* of the law'. So that this bloody crew would have men *put to death* for using the *only means* left them to save themselves from starvation! (11.12.1830)

The violent emphases of this language compare well with the glozing qualifiers, the insidious and apparently reasonable incitements, of the ruling-class paper.

Yet Cobbett's success as a particular kind of journalist had an ironic sequel. The proposed form of the *Register*, with its regular and systematic information, was only ever partly achieved, and in later years the repressive Stamp Acts made popular *newspapers* very difficult to publish, pushing radical journalism towards pamphlets of opinion. Since Cobbett had begun writing in just this form, of which he was always a master, it did not cramp his style, but it did influence the character of radical journalism. During the period of open repression, Cobbett and other radicals, in spite of their great difficulties, could compete very well with the organs of established opinion. But then two things changed.

First, through steam-mechanical printing and railway distribution, the levels of possible circulation and then of necessary capitalisation rose rapidly. The radical papers found themselves in an increasingly unequal competition, but at the same time the ruling-class papers were able to establish a relative independence from governments of the day. The bought and bribed Press of the repressive period was succeeded by increasingly successful commercial enterprises of a new kind, which eventually established themselves not only as establishment but as new forms of *popular* papers.

Secondly, the content of journalism broadened on this base: faster and more regular news, systematic current information and record of every kind. Opinion was still wrapped in this, but then looked very different from the relatively unwrapped opinion which became the predominant content of the undercapitalised and low-circulation radical Press. For a generation radical opinion was joined, in some cases, by systematic scandal and sensation, especially in the new popular Sunday papers. These sold more than the daily papers, but by the end of the century most of the radical politics had long disappeared from them, while the scandal and sensation remained. Such papers, and the papers of systematic news and information, were no longer the simple creatures of ministries and factions which Cobbett had attacked. But they were necessarily, by their increasingly concentrated ownership, parts of the economic and social system which radical opinion was attacking. The Cobbett legacy of hard campaigning opinion was honourably continued, but typically in papers which had only this, and none of the other developed journalistic elements, to recommend them.

In a time of great crisis which was also a time of limited institutional politics, Cobbett's kind of journalism, based in an old pamphleteering tradition and in the current form of the 'open letter', with its directly personalising reference and address, succeeded to an extraordinary extent. But already in his last years the forms of politics, and even more the whole nature of the economy and the society, were changing in unprecedented ways. Cobbett did more than most ten men could have done to intervene in the forms and to explain the changes. But ahead of him there was a different crisis, of long-run information and of beliefs. It is here, perhaps, that his contradictory opinions on education can enter, under different circumstances, into a very damaging combination with the vigour and style of his polemics.

Cobbett was in no real sense anti-intellectual. He opposed some important intellectual forms mainly because of the social uses to which they were indeed being put. He fought very hard to disseminate useful information and to extend public reasoning and argument. But the dominant polemical style (which ran through his major changes of opinion) could, deprived of the exposure and extremity which in his great years justified it, not only be seen as rant (especially in comparison with the smoothed bias of established opinion), but by inattentive imitation actually become rant.

Thus the politics of the radical and labour movements, buoyed up by the evident justice of their causes, could appear, as often in Cobbett, to become autonomous: the angry answer, sufficient only in its anger, to starvation and repression. These movements had to learn, beyond Cobbett, the need for popular education, including book-learning, if change and the means of change were to be understood. In doing so they often forgot the real warnings, about content and control, which Cobbett had entwined with his prohibitions and discouragements. Eventually, indeed, they forgot, disastrously, the autonomy on which he had insisted. Many forgot the force of his distinction, even where negatively used, between education as a received curriculum, always then anchored to specific social perspectives designed to maintain the existing social system, and education as the active means of understanding and changing their real conditions. In Cobbett himself all these difficult points are in effect inextricable. It does no honour to him to continue the confusions.

3 Issues

One sense of history requires that we see Cobbett in his time: 'in his period'. We then study his campaigns in relation to the immediate conditions and events that provoked them. We study his ideas within the thinking and prejudices of his day. We applaud and apologise within this time-bound perspective.

One sense of writing requires that we see Cobbett both in his time and in ours. His uses of language belong to his time: the condition of English in the early nineteenth century; the social relations within which he developed particular uses – those distinctive combinations of formality and colloquial polemic.

> '*Coarse as neck beef!*' will growl out some Englishman, who has filled his bags by oppressions of the poor; or, some other one, who, feeling in his very bones and marrow an instinctive horror of *work*, is desperately bent on getting *a share of the taxes*. (24.5.1828)

This is from a late Open Letter, but the style is more generally characteristic. The hard colloquialism is placed, emphatically, at the beginning of the sentence, necessitating subsequent inversion of the normal grammatical order (but see the diminished effect if the 'normal' order is restored). At the same time, there is a careful formality in the semi-colon, the heavy commas, and the relatively abstract phrase 'some other one'. *Bags* and *bones and marrow* are from everyday speech; *oppressions of the poor*, *instinctive* and *desperately bent* from the written page. The punching italics, which Cobbett always used very heavily, belong to a style of assertive address, in effect as an oral notation, yet the structure of the formal eighteenth- and early-nineteenth-century sentence is basically retained, both in syntax and in rhythm. Over his wide range there are many forms of writing, but this is his most specific. It is in his grafting of colloquial phrases and oral emphases on to the still formal strengths of the consciously public address of his period that his most distinctive practice can be recognised and defined. Pointing forward, this combination is still extraordinarily readable. Much of his writing still directly engages us: never irrespective of his time but not bound by it either. There are different preferences: for the rural rider; for the democratic pamphleteer; for the practical countryman. Yet all these as writer: the writing outlasting its occasions.

These are reasonable senses of both history and writing. But there are other senses, which ought now to be explored. There is a sense of history as connecting rather than separating his time and ours. Not then this period and that, but a common country, in an actual succession, inheritance, of lives. And not then writing as style: the critical or textual study; but writing as a practice, within this country and inheritance: the giving and taking of energy, in this durable form, to attempt or actually to make new kinds of relationship. William Cobbett as a contributor, in this continuing life.

Cobbett and Old England

Cobbett can be preserved in amber as the figure of what is called Old England. In one way not unjustly: he offered himself, in terms, as its spokesman. To this specific claim, for the happy rural England of his boyhood, can be added all the particulars: of the smell of baking bread, the glow of the cheek at the oven; of the taste of spring water, as against hard water, in beer; of the look of a goose from the stubble, against a green goose; of fine young oaks along the Weald, of the beauty and usefulness of ash trees; of the bright water meadows by the Ouse, the clouds above the trees of Penyard Hill, the flocks of sheep to Appleshaw fair; nuts and apples at Newbury, wildfowl at Petersfield, nightingales at Chilworth; white wheat on the clay, 'dying of a good colour' (R 30.7.1823).

Old England? But there is nothing particularly old about these things that Cobbett saw and touched and tasted. Things like them, or often their actual successors, are still there and accessible. In what proportions can be argued about, but still the quickest way to them is on our feet and not through spectacles at Cobbett. That we shall see other, less pleasant things on the way is not in question. So did Cobbett: 'two entire miles of stock-jobbers' houses on this one road'; 'all is bleak and comfortless; and, just on the most dreary part of this most dreary scene, stands almost opportunely, "*Caxton* Gibbet", tendering its friendly one arm to the passers-by'; 'dwellings ... little better than pig-beds ... wretched hovels'; 'a group of women labourers ... some very pretty girls, but ragged as colts and pale as ashes'; 'a county bridewell standing on the very spot where stood the abbey which was founded and endowed by Alfred'; 'nabobs, negro-drivers, generals, admirals, governors, commissaries, contractors, pensioners, sinecurists, commissioners, loan-jobbers, lottery-dealers, bankers, stock-jobbers; not to mention the long and *black list* in gowns and three-tailed wigs ... few good houses not in possession of one or the other of these' (R 8.1.1822; 22.1.1822; 7.11.1821; 6.11.1821; 30.10.1825; 21.11.1821).

Old England? Cobbett's England, for all its natural beauties and simple pleasures, was the place where 'the *Thing*' (24.7.1830) had happened, where the body of the land had been deformed by the 'monstrous Wen' (22.2.1823) of London. To go back, as he did, to the Old England of his boyhood, is to find Goldsmith standing and pondering: 'I see the rural virtues leave the land.' This sense of loss and wistful retrospect can be traced far back. Cobbett offered his own interpretation, for his own time. If he is the voice of anything that can be called, for rhetorical purposes, Old England, he is also in that act the voice of protest against finance capital, imperialism and the aristocratic State, and the voice of encouragement of working-class organisation, democratic protest and popular defiance. It is only by falsifying selection that he can be enrolled for that now common nostalgia, in which an image of old rural England is emblazoned against the actual people of England, often by the literal descendants of the nabobs, negro-drivers, generals, admirals, governors, commissioners, bankers, stock-jobbers and lawyers.

In this tendency Cobbett is appropriated and deflected. In

another, very different tendency he is patted on the head. A good radical, a good democrat, but he did not understand what was happening, in the new industrial England. He is thus at once a radical and a reactionary: a resister of progress and yet a spokesman for popular rights. A good brave old chap, who lived just before modernity.

Appropriation can be detected. Patronage is more of a problem. In fact an examination of the issues involved in the 'radical yet reactionary', 'democratic but pre-modern' diagnosis takes us into some of the most difficult social analysis of the epoch that extends from Cobbett's time to our own.

Cobbett and the new England

Cobbett tied together his own package of ideas. But he was doing this at a time when a much larger package of events was being put together, as a transforming history. Once this package had been tied, plenty of people were ready to put labels on it. 'Modern England'; 'Industrial England'; 'Industrial-Capitalist England'; 'Imperial England'. There could be argument about the labels, but most of it occurred within a sense of an achieved state, or of an achieved state from which the next stage of achievement was fairly obvious. Cobbett, the good old chap, had lived just before these achievements. He could be a friend in spirit, but he was not on our road.

This is all quite convincing until we look up and notice that we no longer have this achieved state, and that the next stage of achievement is far from obvious. It is not clear whether this will affect our view of Cobbett. What it seems bound to affect is our confidence in the labels, and in the diagnoses and opinions that come with them. Or, to put it another way, we may find that the transforming history is not only a package of *events*. Perhaps our *minds*, also, were packed and wrapped in the same bundle. When we thought we were labelling, we were seeing only parts of the package, from inside.

Yet, if this is so, it is improbable that Cobbett can help us get out. The years and the events have all quite materially happened. Their products, of every kind, are thick on the ground.

So there can be no indulgent trailing after Cobbett's ghost; no lifting of his bones. What we can actually learn from him is different, and less flattering: what it is like to be living through a time when an old social order is visibly breaking up but when we do not have the advantage of hindsight to show us the new social order that is succeeding it. This uncertain and restless condition is very characteristic of the most concerned and most passionate men of Cobbett's own day. It is marked, paradoxically, by intense and radical convictions: of the evils of the time, of the depths of its disturbances; of the new things that must happen, the new life that is coming through. In Cobbett and Blake, in Shelley and Carlyle, for all their individual differences, there is this characteristic intensity of denunciation of what is happening in their world, and also this characteristic confidence that these evils cannot last, that something radically new must come. Yet what came as new, whatever else may be said of it, was not within their line of vision at all; indeed was in many of its elements only an intensification of what they had denounced.

We may think we now understand this condition. There was abundant evidence that matters were very wrong. Their pity for the victims of these wrongs, their contempt for the orthodox apologias and reconciliations, and for the more glaring and rampant indifferences and cruelties, ran deep. But what had they to offer against these? Radical remedies, of one kind or another: the revival of almost lost virtues; renewal from the more lasting sources of life. This is where they divided, in spirit and in detail, but what remains common in them is the conviction that things could not go on as they were. This can be respected in isolation, as the wrongs are recalled. But what in fact takes over is a different consciousness: that the forces which were then coming through, forces which in general they opposed, were in fact the waves of the future: waves that would break on the shore of modernity, run clear to where we now stand. So we are asked to look back at them as struggling with currents, with tides, which they did not understand; look back from where *we* are, on land.

Yet it must at last be obvious that wherever we may now be,

we are not on firm ground. And then the problem is not the recognition that matters are again very wrong. That comes to most of us, and so do the contemporary apologias and reconciliations; so also, heavy around us, the indifferences and the cruelties. What is really problematic is the nature of our responses. The revival of almost lost virtues? Renewal from the more lasting sources of life? But if we have any sense of history we cannot, as we consider these, forget the picture we have been given: of those earlier people who were struggling, bravely enough, with forces they did not understand. We may suppose we can exempt ourselves from this likely deficiency. Indeed that vanity is often the condition of hope. But what we can not reasonably do is miss the community of situation: an old order breaking up; uncertainty and restlessness, but in these men radical convictions, that certain new things must happen; definitions of these new things in the only available vocabulary — that of the already known and imagined. We are not facing the same world but we have the same kind of problem. This helps us to understand how they really stood, before a future projected, imagined, exhorted but still quite radically unknown. It may also help us to realise how we now really stand.

What was it then that was new?

The central question which Cobbett's period puts to us, and which we may look to him to help us to answer, is this: What was it then that was new?

We have our own important but now standard answer: the Industrial Revolution. Yet what then are we to make of the fact that this was not Cobbett's answer, that he named quite different things? Because he was struggling in currents he did not understand? It is before that simple conclusion that I am suggesting we must hesitate.

The events that we label the Industrial Revolution came in a complex historical package. Yet one of these has been regularly isolated, in the description itself. What is seen as really changing is a method of production.

But 'method of production' covers several distinguishable

facts. We can make one important initial distinction: between changing *forces* of production and changing *relations* of production. It is then interesting to see where Cobbett stands on these initially distinguishable changes.

One false account stands in our way, and Cobbett can help us to get rid of it. It is very widely believed that the new production methods of the Industrial Revolution were imposed on a relatively unchanging, even 'timeless', rural economy. Thus the rural economy is seen as the old order; the industrial economy as the new. But this false contrast can set the argument wrong from the beginning.

The forces of rural production were changing quite rapidly in Cobbett's lifetime, and indeed were already changing significantly in his father's lifetime. The great improvements in stock-breeding were already well under way when he was born. New techniques of earth-moving, of drainage, of deep tillage, were also coming through. Cobbett joined in with these changes, as an eager innovator. He had his own opinions about this technique or that, but in the matter of *forces* of production he was an entire partisan for improvement. He ran his own long campaign for swedes and then mangolds as fodder, and for the introduction of maize. He was continually looking for improvements in the harvesting and treatment of produce, by new devices and machines. He made a good deal of progress in the new skills of the commercial seedsman. And all this is only to say that he was a practical farmer and grower, in the long history of improvement of land and crops and stock which was at a very important stage in his lifetime and which has continued to our own day.

These were improvements in the forces of production of food. But then what is striking is that there was not yet, in his lifetime, a categorical separation of this production as the 'rural economy', with all other production in the 'industrial economy'. Thus he made no initial separation of 'agricultural' and 'industrial' production, of the kind that has become commonplace and misleading. In fact, in his letter to the Nottingham weavers, he placed himself firmly on the side of machinery:

The writers on the side of Corruption are very anxious to inculcate notions *hostile* to machinery ... By machines mankind are able to do that which their own bodily powers would never effect to the same extent ... Every *implement* used by man is a *machine*, machine merely meaning *thing* as contradistinguished from the *hand of man*. (30.11.1816)

This is the material Cobbett: the man who used or saw the use of spade, hatchet, knife, fish-hook, flail, gun, threshing-machine, loom, water-mill. The distinction at this level – as always in fact – is not between 'rural' and 'industrial', but between simple handwork and various stages of the development of 'machines'. With the advantage of hindsight, we can now see the problems of his equation of 'implement' with 'machine'. The threshing-machine, the new looms, the water-mill were more than simple extensions of arm and hand. Other natural forces were being harnessed in ways that separated the 'machine', which could be set to work under its own power, from the 'implement', which was still directly connected to the human body. But the new machines, like the hand-tools, were being applied, as necessary, to 'rural' and 'industrial' production alike.

It was not then the 'machines' in themselves – the standard 'industrial' component of the Industrial Revolution – that Cobbett opposed. On the contrary, as forces of production he in general welcomed them. What he was attacking was quite different, or seemed quite different, and it was happening on the land, in the rural economy, before he saw it also happening in the 'industrial' economy. This was what he saw as a change in the *relations* of production: new kinds of exploitation of labourers by farmers, and of farmers by landlords. He then saw comparable exploitation of spinners and weavers, the new 'industrial' workers, by employers. In neither case did he refer this exploitation primarily to the changing forces of production. Even in one of the hardest cases – the high temperature necessary in mechanical cotton-spinning – what he attacked was keeping people locked up in such heat, without pause, for fourteen hours a day. He could come to think that it would be better, for the general balance of life, if the making of clothes and their materials was kept inside the agricultural economy. But this was primarily a social argument. He put human relations and human satisfactions first, and saw technical improvements, including machines, as necessary and useful if they served these ends. When they did not, he blamed the relations of production first.

Industrialism and capitalism

This point of view, so clear in Cobbett, takes us at once into the most difficult area of the general argument. Most of us now believe that changes in the forces of production necessarily bring with them changes in the relations of production. Thus whether, as in one influential tradition, we attack the industrial revolution as destroying a more humane social order, or whether, in the dominant view, we see it as inevitable progress, with great costs but with greater benefits, we accept the linkage between forces and relations of production as basic.

The new machines required new factories, which required new industrial towns. That is the easier part of the linkage. There is of course another. The new machines required new capital, which required new relations between a class of capitalist employers and a class of industrial wage-labourers. In fact both parts of this linkage happened together, historically. It is then easy to believe that both parts were inevitable, but this can mean two different things.

It can mean that the development of industrial production and of industrial capitalism were inevitably linked, in the social and historical conditions in which both developed. Or it can mean that industrial production and industrial capitalism are linked as such, though the forms of either may change. This second position has one specific difficulty. How is industrial capitalism to be opposed, in its specific and systematic kinds of exploitation, if it is linked in this way to industrial production as such?

In fact some influential opponents of industrial capitalism have drifted, repeatedly, to a rejection of industrial production. Cobbett, implausibly, but more plausibly Carlyle, Ruskin,

William Morris and others have been enrolled in this rejection. The recovery, as it is called, of a more humane social order involves at least the limitation, often the cancellation, of the processes of industrial production.

Meanwhile others, in mainline socialism, though often believing, as a matter of principle, that there is a necessary linkage between particular forces and particular relations of production, propose to retain and develop, for good reasons, the new and developing forces of production, but at the same time to transform the relations of production. In some of their characteristic early attempts, the linkage has seemed to assert itself. Ownership of the means of production has been changed, to the State or to public boards, but the immediate *relations* of production, under the persistent imperatives of the *forces* of production, have not been similarly changed: there is still an effective class of employers and an effective class of wage-earners. Has the basic linkage then proved too strong?

Production and the State

Cobbett did not cast his own arguments in terms of any necessary linkage between forces and relations of production. This may well have been because he saw comparatively little of the new ways in which they were coming together, in the factories and the mills, the ironworks and the mines. He judged what he saw mainly in terms of the immediate physical conditions of the workers, which could be directly compared with the varying physical conditions of labourers in the fields and woods and on the roads. It was in any case still early for anyone to see the factory *system* in anything like its full development. Many people still believed that the new type of work would occupy only a limited sector of the economy, and it was not until the second half of the century that it clearly came through as dominant.

It can then be said, in a local truth, that Cobbett did not understand the new industrialism, and that his mind was still held by the ideas of the old rural economy. But this is to measure him by a later perspective which may in itself be very much too simple. It is a measure in terms primarily of the changing forces of production, and of changing relations of production as mainly physically derived from these: the concentration of workers in mills and factories as against the relatively scattered domestic workers, outworkers and artisans. That is in itself a major change, in its effects on the structures of families and settlements, but it is only part of the full changes in relations of production. For these are not only physical and communal; they are also, in the full sense, economic.

Cobbett is so often remembered for what he saw in physical terms, whether of land or of labour, that it is easy to forget that he gave a great deal of time, over thirty years, to writing about money, and about the connections he saw between the financial system, the political State, and their combined effects on the condition of the country. Though he supported several other kinds of reform, he continued to believe that it was in this area that the most fundamental reforms were necessary. It was this 'accursed system' which was the deepest cause of the suffering and disorder. Moreover it was not merely a monetary and financial system; it was a monetary and financial system which had produced a particular kind of political State.

It is here that the problems of the relations between 'industrialism' and 'capitalism' are at their most acute. Cobbett had no theory of capitalism, in its mature industrial forms, and his specific writings about money – his long campaigns for gold against paper – can be seen as merely antiquated. But it is at least worth considering whether he did not get hold, if incompletely, of a larger system in which the relations between the money market and the political order were close and decisive. If we do not foreshorten capitalism to 'industrialism' or 'industrial capitalism', this may be easier to see.

Cobbett began, in 1803, by attacking the funding system and the National Debt. These were, at the time, increasing rapidly, as a way of financing the war against France. Cobbett's early arguments about paper money and inflation soon broadened to an argument in which he asserted a direct relation between the rise of a new class of fund- and stock-holders and an increase

in new kinds of poverty. What were called the Bank of England
and the National Debt had begun in the 1690s, when a group of
private financiers, lending money to the government, had
gained a privileged position which deformed all subsequent
notions of the public or national interest.

> We have so long called the thing a Debt; we have so long
> called the funds *property*; we have so long talked of a
> *mortgage* which the Fundholders have upon the Nation; we
> have so long called the Fundholders *Creditors*; that, at last,
> we have confounded a matter of State with a private trans-
> action; two things wholly distinct in their origin, in their
> progress, and in all their bearing and effects. (17.2.1821)

Cobbett repeatedly argued for reducing or cancelling payment
of interest on this so-called 'National' debt, as a way of relieving
the burden it placed on productive land and labour: 'The *land*,
of itself, does not pay a fifth part of the interest of the Debt.
The rest is raised from *labour* of various sorts. It is taken out of
wages'. Thus the real national interest is repeatedly set aside in
the name of this false National Interest.

> As to this national *Debt*, as it is called, it is just and proper
> never to pay another farthing of interest upon it, if the good
> of the whole nation, taking one part with another, require a
> cessation of such payment. The Fundholder is not to be
> thought of for a *moment*, if the prosperity and happiness of
> the Nation demand that the interest should no longer be paid.
> What a monstrous idea, that a *Nation* is to be bound to it's
> ruin by individuals!

Yet this, Cobbett argued, was essentially what was happening.
Through manipulation of the money market, and through its
intricate interlocking with the central processes of government,
the real interests of the nation were being systematically set
aside, to the benefit only of the dealers in money. 'Ours is essentially a stockjobbing government. All its favours are reserved
for the crew who deal in money' (12.7.1823). It was by the manipulation of money that the rural economy had been changed.

The breaking up of the Commons and Downs was a natural effect of the forced increase of money; and, in this way, amongst the rest, that increase worked detriment to the labourer. It was out of his bones that the means came. It was the *deduction made from him by the rise of prices* and by the *not-rise of his wages*: it was the means thus raised that enclosed the Commons and Downs. (5.5.1821)

Parliament, in this as in so much else, was merely the willing tool of the financial system, which was effectively the real government of the country.

The link between the political government, ostensibly serving the general interests of the people, and the political government as agent and creature of the system of loans and funding, was of course taxation. This was where the government pretended to act in the common interest but actually acted in the interest of bondholders, bankers and stockjobbers.

I do not say, that *no taxes* ought to be collected ... In a large community of men, there must be laws to protect the weak against the strong; there must be administrators of the laws; there must be persons to hold communications with foreign powers; there must be, in case of necessary wars, a public force to carry on such wars. All these require taxes of some sort; but, when the load of taxes becomes so heavy as to produce *general misery* amongst all those who pay and who do not receive taxes, then it is that taxes become an enormous evil. This is our state at present. It is the sum taken from those who labour to be given to those who do not labour, which has produced all our present misery. (30.11.1816)

Who were those who did not labour? The many thousands of government sinecurists, where political and financial privilege came together. Then

twenty thousand parsons; more than twenty thousand stock-brokers and stockjobbers perhaps; forty or fifty thousand tax-gatherers; thousands upon thousands of military and naval officers in full pay; in addition to all these, here are

thousands upon thousands of pairs of this Dead Weight, all
busily engaged in breeding gentlemen and ladies . . . all receiv-
ing a *premium for breeding*! (R 8.8.1823)

This was at once a political and a social system: the ruling class
and its dependants. And the most important thing about it was
that it was not productive; that it was a burden carried, through
taxation, on the backs of the real producers. The false political
and social system was then the direct result of a false system of
money, which had been allowed to become dominant. The
system treated money transactions as productive, and their
consequences as obligatory social relations. But

that paper-money, and, indeed, that money of no sort, can
create any thing valuable, is evident; and that it cannot *cause*
it to be created, on a general scale, is also evident; for, all
valuable things arise from *labour*, and, if an addition to the
quantity of money sets labour in motion in one place, it draws
it from another place; that is all that it does. If its nature and
operation be such as to cause new and fine houses and car-
riages and 'grand dinners' to make their appearance, it takes
away the means of furnishing the houses of the most numerous class, robs them of their bedding, their food, their drink
and their raiment. Nothing is *created* by it. It is not value in
itself; but merely the *measure of value*, and the means of
removing valuable things from one possessor to another.
(26.5.1821)

Thus, before industrial capitalism had at all generally
developed in Britain, and before the effects of changes in the
forces of production could show up in immediate changes in the
relations of production, there was what Cobbett saw as the
decisive and systematic relation of all production to the money
market, in which money itself had been changed from a measure
of value to a pseudo-commodity, from which those who dealt in
it, and the political system which was entwined with it, gained
more wealth than real producers of any kind. It was not only the
disproportion that was evil. It was that this ruling system, and

its embodiment in the State, crippled real production and the general prosperity which it would otherwise bring.

The ruling system vindicated?

This is a very different and much harder position than the more familiar view of the Industrial Revolution in terms of directly increased production. The argument usually jams at that point, with it being said on the one hand that the conditions of the early industrial workers and their new towns were appalling, and on the other hand that the wealth of the nation was very greatly increased, forming a basis for all subsequent prosperity. Since each of these propositions is true, there seems to be little more to say. The prosperity continued, and came to be more fairly distributed (in alternative versions, because of the increasing prosperity, or because the workers through their unions could get more). Either way, there is an end of it. It happened, and people like Cobbett look about as relevant as Canute. Indeed there is now a fashionable model in which many different kinds of critics of the actual processes of the Industrial Revolution are lumped together as literary sentimentalists, while a tougher breed insist that it was all necessary and (in spite of some early and perhaps some later blemishes) right.

This model is misleading in many respects: most notably in the way it confuses quite different arguments, as if those who pointed to the damaging conditions of the industrial workers, to their low pay, to the conditions of their housing and towns, to the effects on health and environment of specific industrial processes, were of a piece with those who wanted to live at a comfortable distance from all real work, in some fantasy of funded simplicity. It is Cobbett more than anyone who can prevent this fashionable trick being played, as it is now from almost all quarters. For the question he raises is whether the fundamental argument can take place at all in these familiar but limited terms. It is a question which strikes with great force within a changed situation: in which the argument is not occurring within conditions of general industrial prosperity — the supposed baseline of the subsequently conflicting views — but within conditions of general and in some views irreversible industrial decline.

The first element of an answer comes in the point already noted: that the Industrial Revolution was not a sudden imposition on an unchanging or 'timeless' rural economy. The first major capitalist class in England was agrarian: the improving and exploiting landlords who had grown in social and economic power and in increased production from the late seventeenth century through to Cobbett's own day. Alongside these was a growing class of merchants, already heavily involved not only in internal but in external trade, including the notorious triangle of slaves, cotton and manufactured goods. The pattern of exploiting employers and exploited labourers was thus already present before the machines turned, and intricately interwoven with it was a pattern of external exploitation and a rapidly extending financial system. Cobbett saw most but not all of this exceptionally complex pattern. He idealised the old land-lords, and saw their dispossession by the merchants and money-men as a disaster, though also largely their own fault. There was indeed some 'dispossession', though often of earlier generations of 'dispossessors', but the more central process was an intricate adjustment, involving new economic objectives and institutions, which produced a relatively successful *because efficiently exploiting* social order.

As an economic process, the Industrial Revolution, in its successive phases, grew from the body of this successful agrarian and mercantile capitalism. It was no simple growth, and there were many internal conflicts of economic and political interest. But for perhaps a century, until the 1870s and 1880s, it was in its turn an exceptionally successful system. It produced great relative economic power and wealth in the 'nation', to be sure at the cost of the relative poverty of the majority of the nation's inhabitants. It appeared wholly to outdistance, and to make irrelevant, the widespread complaints that it was cruel, destructive and unnatural. Even Cobbett's great voice faded to an antique mumble, which could be safely disregarded by all practical men.

One other kind of voice did not fade, but became ever louder: that of the organising and organised labour movement, which had been forced to new relations and new consciousness by the experience of new kinds of aggregated work in mills and factories, ironworks and mines. Yet though this voice had behind it the long experience and recurrent protests of the rural labourers and the craftsmen and artisans, it was necessarily a different voice: systematically addressed, as can be heard to this day, to its immediate enemies, its direct employers. The element of socialism which grew, unevenly and always with confusions and difficulties, within this labour movement, had of course much wider objects of address: to the whole social order, to its politics, economy and external relations. Yet it came to be believed that the verbal and often actual affiliations between the labour movement and socialism were necessary and even organic: not that they had to be made, but that they were given.

Thus not only the developed labour movement, but also most forms of developed radicalism and of the socialism conceived within these influences, could look back at an earlier history and its arguments with confidence and even complacency. Modern Britain, this successful industrial and commercial concern, could be reformed, even radically, in its own terms. Social relations could be softened and harmonised; industrial relations regulated and improved; the wealth more equally shared and applied to new kinds of welfare. It was a programme which made the old railers and the new alien theorists alike redundant. Great Britain Ltd would become Great Britain, the Modern and Caring Society. Out of its own guts.

It cannot be Cobbett who shows us the deficiencies of this programme. They are being shown more directly, in the rapidly breaking crisis of forces and relations which are quite beyond this perspective. It has in fact been a long crisis, but it has now reached the point where it is possible for orthodox voices to speak of the forced 'de-industrialisation' of Britain; where the problems of the financial system and its management have come to dominate economic and political argument; where settled and confident institutions and provisions are being disturbed and broken by financial emergencies; where Great Britain in either of its versions exports capital and imports weapons of mass destruction, while settling to an apparently unending period of widespread unemployment and redundancy.

It equally cannot be Cobbett who shows us any way out of this deep failure. But at least he can remind us of factors which that confident orthodox perspective (as confident on one side as the other of the party lines conceived within it) not only left out but often actually repressed from consciousness. There are three of these factors: we can consider the two most easily separable first.

Finance capital and Empire

Cobbett undoubtedly exaggerated the importance of the financial system in the politics and economics of his day. It was especially prominent in the conduct of the wars against France, but it was still only part of a much more broadly based system. What he did not exaggerate was the potential and probably inherent conflict between such a financial system and necessary production. It is easy to see, as we follow the story down, that much more flexible forms of money and credit were possible, without the ruin he so often predicted. It is also clear that the use of such a financial system was a central element in the great increases in industrial production, as in the increases in agricultural production which had preceded it. But then, if we are to follow the story, we have to follow the whole story.

What Cobbett had identified was a form of ruling class, and an attendant form of State power, which was centred on income from money, in any of its possible kinds, and on the use of this income for its own social purposes, in power and display and consumption: a class and a State which saw production as means to these ends, rather than to the sustained prosperity of its own land and people. If these different ends coincided, so much the better. But if they came into conflict, there would be no real doubt which would be chosen. This is the English class and the English State which would eventually and quite openly under-invest in its own land, its own people, its own industries, but send capital flying to any spot in the world which would yield a higher money income, to continue to finance its ever more conspicuous consumption, display and power.

Again there is a problem of perspective. Cobbett attacked the early ventures into Empire. For example:

> The recent intelligence from India, or 'our Empire in the East', is of a gloomy complexion, in my sight, only inasmuch as it gives an account of the loss of a great number of English officers and soldiers. It may serve to make men reflect justly on the nature of the wars we carry on in India; and may lead them to the conclusion, so much to be desired, that the possession of that country is a terrible evil. This, it seems, is to be *the last* war; but, we have been told the same thing for more than thirty years past. There is a constant, never-ceasing war in India. There is not always actual fighting; but, there are always going on preparations for fighting. What right, in God's name, what right have we to do this? How is it possible for us to justify our conduct, upon any principle of morality? ... We must be actuated by a sheer love of gain; a sheer love of plunder. (16.4.1808)

An antique voice? The trouble is that for more than a century it could seem so, as the wealth poured in, to that ruling class and beyond it, from India, from the Caribbean, from Africa. A State more gross and insolent than anything even Cobbett could have conceived grew on that wealth, raising beneath it subordinate classes of soldiers and officials, corrupting its own people with assumptions of everlasting privileged advantage. And at the end of it, after 'the last' or almost the last war, with so much blood spilled, what? A system so oriented to the combined pursuit of unearned wealth and military power that it had virtually forgotten its own land and industries, and radically deflected its own people's skills and desires. In the place of both it had created a fantasy of England: top bulldog; green and pleasant land; peace-loving. It even had the insolence, and the ignorance, to enrol a censored version of Cobbett in this fantasy.

But if Empire eventually ended, the system of finance capital did not. It is now very different in scale and kind from that which Cobbett saw forming, but if he were able to see the great congress of international bankers, stockbrokers and jobbers, investment directors, pension-fund and insurance managers, commodity speculators, financial advisers and journalists, he would recognise the types. And he would certainly, and justly, say much the same things about the relations between this established and commanding system, through which necessary production has to fight its way, and the needs and interests of a native land and its working people.

It has been said that when he railed against the fund-drawers and tax-eaters he showed his *petit-bourgeois* ideology: the interests of small producers against both State and High Finance. This is true but not the most relevant truth. There can be no reasonable position about a tax-eating State until it is fully clear who is benefiting from the taxes: a position we are still far from having reached, since they are bundled together and in practice indistinguishable, used for so diverse a range of actual purposes. As for High Finance, there is a continuing common interest against it, between small producers and working people of all kinds: a common interest that has often been lost because it has been deflected, in different directions, towards a merely abstract State. Cobbett's whole and still relevant point is that, in their developed and developing forms, the ruling-class State and the financial system are aspects of the same social order, against which wide and diverse majorities of the people must be urgently formed.

The culture of the rentier

'Nobody owes the British people a living,' governments now regularly tell the British people. This astounding revelation is addressed to people for whom, in majority, the problem has always been how to make and keep a living through successive crises of economic disorganisation and war. It is addressed to hard-working people by the representatives of a system which has at best made the results of hard work uncertain and at worst nullified and squandered them. But there is a deeper irony than that. The address is made by the representatives of a system which insists that the possessors of capital and of privilege are, precisely, owed a living by everybody else. This no doubt accounts for the sense of a novel truth, as it forms in their mouths. For it is no surprise to anybody else. It was only the great proprietors of the 'National Debt' and the Funds who believed and took steps to ensure that a living was owed to them. It was a debt, as we have seen, which Cobbett wanted to repudiate, in the interests of the real nation.

The position has a continuing significance, beyond the more immediate changes of scale and condition. What Cobbett was attacking was the culture of the *rentier*: the whole way of life based on profit from the work of others. This is why he must never be confused with that distaste for industry, that cultivated superiority to all the ordinary forms of work, which flourished in England within a *rentier* and later a *rentier*-bureaucratic culture. (It is significant that we have to use foreign loan-words for these central English facts: those who lived here on income from rents and shares and bonds, based on production in Britain and over half the world, succeeded in describing themselves and getting others to describe them as 'persons of rank and title', ladies and gentlemen, people of *independent* means!)

But then the argument becomes complex, for the most evident alternative to the *rentiers* were the on-the-spot industrial employers, the improving and rationalising engineers and technicians, the hard-driving distributors. Of course the 'people of independent means' kept putting them down, socially and culturally. All but a few came in fact to measure their success, or their children's success, by entry into the *rentier* culture: into its titles, country houses, styles and forms of education. Moreover the privileged culture, for its own security, was prepared to let them in, on these terms. In deepening economic crises these still active producers from time to time recover their nerve, speak for their own culture, call for the modernisation of Britain. The complexity is then their indignation that most of the working people of Britain do not immediately join them. As a result, such modernisers are usually much more indignant about, say, trade unions than about the archaic State forms and the outward-investing institutions of finance capital which have been their permanent enemies.

Yet, quite apart from the spell cast on most of the people by the forms of the *rentier* culture, centred on the adapted monarchy, most working people have good reason to distrust this more thrusting and productive sector. As Cobbett was one of the first to record, the dislocation of their lives – their places of work, their communities, their families, their traditional working skills – by just such thrusting entrepreneurs was severe and prolonged. The men who had planned the canals abandoned them for the railways and then largely abandoned the railways for the roads; tore the land for coal and then switched to oil; improved productivity, in a thousand trades, by rationalising a majority of workers into redundancy. All their urgent programmes are for more of the same: a prolonged statistical crowing that more and more workers have been got rid of, 'overmanning' reduced. Sighing among the debris of one worked-out area and trade after another, the working people of Britain have no evident cause to join in on these terms. Indeed they are much more likely to join in goggling at the latest *rentier* fantasy of the 'good old days'.

This cultural deadlock in Britain has of course to be broken in contemporary terms. Yet it is reasonable to see Cobbett, from his distance, as a contributor to breaking it. This is so in two respects: in the quality of his concern for the land, and in his primary concern for working people and their families.

Remembering the long celebration of the early phases of the Industrial Revolution, it is ironic to notice that agriculture is now one of the few efficient productive enterprises in Britain, and that it is in the factories and the mills that there are now the most unmistakeable signs of decline. The 'modern' economy, which outdated Cobbett, is now itself distinctly old. It is impossible not to smile a little as the despised and neglected 'rural economy' produces three-quarters of the food of a vastly greater population, long after it too was cast for redundancy, as the factories and mills poured out goods to pay for cheap food from elsewhere. Yet looking closer checks the smile. The improved efficiency of food production would have been greatly to Cobbett's taste, but he would have seen at once how closely it has been tied up with the drastic reduction and forcing-out of small farmers and labourers – those millions then, those many more millions since – who had to go to the cities where there is 'plenty of work'! He would have seen also the realities of the development of agribusiness, especially in the arable counties, based on relatively large and often external capital, with land rents thoroughly integrated into the *rentier* system and with the wages of farm labourers still among the lowest in the whole economy. This is not the 'rural economy' he recommended, nor of course can his kind of rural economy by any means be reconstructed.

Yet there is this material link: that Cobbett looked, not at the 'rural areas' or at the 'countryside', which are *rentier* terms, but at variable actual land and its uses. He began, as any sane social thinker must, from the specific material resources and possibilities of the land on which his people are settled. He could be wrong, as anyone can be wrong, in specific cases, but it is this nature and foundation of his thinking which remains relevant. The deepest damage done by the long epoch of finance capital and Empire – deeper because more permanent than even the debris of the worked-out areas of the early Industrial Revolution – is a fundamental alienation from the means and resources of actual living. The imperialist exploiters and looters have this physical sense all right, but in other people's lands. Their beneficiaries, back home, see only money and consumption and style; their actual land is more typically a place for them to play, refresh themselves in.

What is now called ecology has a friend in Cobbett, but within that highly varied movement there are crucial distinctions. His strongly physical sense of maintaining and using available resources survives the many local changes of actual processes. It is not his specific recipes (some still good; some, as in the case of fat pigs, absurd) which count. That would be a style of romantic revival, finding a quick home in the *rentier* culture. It is a more general and harder kind of understanding physical possibilities and limits, putting the use and care and renewal of resources first.

Yet not in those familiar terms *first*: that is the trap which is continually sprung. Always the first physical facts and resources in Cobbett are *people*: 'The girls at work in the fields (always my standard)' (R 8.11.1821). This is not the abstract and sentimental 'ecology' ('conservation', 'preservation') which has been spreading so fast through the *rentier* culture: a way of seeing which is always willing to subordinate people, other people, and their immediate physical needs. All his life Cobbett was trying, through many prejudices and difficulties, to put people first. It seems so commonplace a position. Hardly anyone, in general terms, would dissent from it.

But what Cobbett started from, and then through many changes had to struggle to keep clear, was the overriding sense of an arbitrary selection among people. If any such selection is happening, for whatever reason, talk of 'putting people first' or of 'respect for the individual' quickly becomes cant. It was the rare full sense of 'putting people first' which founded his social position. It was what set him against the old order of a few to be served, of the many serving, and against the newer orders in which it was made to appear rational that people had to be repressed or turned off in the name of some greater good. It is impossible that he could have understood the full intricacies and consequences of those new orders that were still just forming. Often he lurched back to what he was used to or what he could by old expectations predict. But at the centre, within what he could see of his time and world, there was this unshakeable principle of prosperity as the well-being of all honest people and their families, and as its obverse his terrible anger at all those who repressed, exploited or despised them. He could be angry that a harvest could be described as producing 'redundancy'. He would be much more angry to hear millions of people now described as 'redundant' by an economic system, claiming the criterion of 'efficiency', which indeed logically ends by making most human beings redundant. 'Nobody owes the British people a living.' 'Nobody will provide the British people with a living.' *Overmanning!* QED.

Work

There is, however, a further irony which would have been not at all to his taste. The improvements in production, which he was beginning to see, have indeed developed so far that in the industrial countries most necessary commodities – and certainly all those on Cobbett's scale of sufficiency – can be produced by a relatively small fraction of the working population. In his own time he believed that people released from one kind of work, for example by new machinery, could quite easily be found other work. This was never wholly true, but the belief in transfer remained strong, through all the generations of increasing population, sustained by the advantages of the early industrial and imperial systems. Now, as the decline of these systems has worked through in Britain, alongside further rapid reductions in the number of immediately necessary workers, the crisis which is cruelly interpreted as 'redundancy' is in one form or another inevitable.

Cobbett fought against recognising anything of the kind. This is one source of his fantasies about the larger population of medieval England. It underlies his deep hostility to schemes of emigration, cold enough in their immediate forms but in the end, past their first generations, fortunate for all those who in fact went. It jars, in him and others, with an interest in efficient production, eventually forcing many humane people into deliberately regressive economic ideas, trying to recover some Old England.

As a general problem it is inevitably complex, but one of its most significant difficulties is that, at certain key points, it collides with what is in many ways the strongest form of Cobbett's social personality, and can then release – if not in him then in others like him – some irrelevant and even dangerous feelings. For even in the mature Cobbett a very different social figure is latent: the sergeant-major, the exacting small employer, the hard-working, quarrelsome and aggressive self-made man (a domineering figure which is actual in his later family life). Add to that the impatience with much education, the contempt for the 'comforting' system, and you have a social type which keeps appearing but which is at its most frustrated and dangerous when deep underlying changes make the apparently simple virtue of hard work questionable.

Of course, even in Cobbett's terms, there is more to say. Redundant production or producers there may be, in the old industrial countries, but there are now more people in absolute poverty, in the world of the late twentieth century, than there were people of all conditions in the world of Cobbett's lifetime. His kind of analysis, of the concentration of wealth, by political power and the financial system, sustaining and actually creating poverty and pauperism elsewhere, can be applied to our world as he applied it to his England. It is true that this means surpassing his strong and directive sense of the prosperity of his *own* people, his *native* land: that necessary attachment which in altered conditions can turn ugly. But the world system which creates, simultaneously, over- and under-development, concentrated wealth and concentrated poverty, heavy military expenditure, financial manipulation and spectacular *rentier* consumption, has a true lineage from the national system which he spent a lifetime attacking. Still, while this negative analysis will hold, his positive recommendations can float away in the air.

It is in thinking about the nature of work that Cobbett is furthest from us. His powerful and necessary respect for physical labour can be too easily translated, in different conditions, into an idealisation of 'hard work'. We have to look at the lights burning late in the offices of the political manipulators and the financial schemers to remember how little necessary correlation there may be between long effort and useful work. Correspondingly, we have to look at 'production' beyond Cobbett's physical terms: not only at the work in families and with children which he conventionally and distantly assigned to women; but at the wider work of producing health, knowledge, community, which are beyond the processes of the independent labourer.

Cobbett broke the link between necessary production and the imposed definitions of 'national wealth' in the terms of a dominant class. In more complex ways we have now to redefine 'production', as a common wealth which is more than necessary commodities, and which has to be based on a deeper and wider version of his own sense of prosperity: the conditions, going far beyond subsistence, of an active, healthy, informed and self-directing community. In that long effort, opposed now as then by the imperatives of the extraction of wealth and privilege, and by the criteria of all narrower definitions of work and productive efficiency, there is not likely to be any genuine redundancy, any shortage of opportunities for useful and constructive effort. Indeed, given such a standard, we can see that 'redundancy' and 'unemployment' are the destructive consequences of the narrow definitions of 'work' and 'wealth' which the capitalist system imposes. They can never be 'cured' within its limited terms. As in Cobbett's time, it is the system that has to be changed.

Changing the system

Cobbett could not have acted so confidently, defied authority so thoroughly, if he had not believed that there were relatively simple remedies, ready to be enacted. We can now see the actual hopelessness of his idea of restoring an older kind of England. We can see also the frustrations of his idea of quickly changing the social and economic order through a reformed Parliament: frustrations that he knew himself in his last years.

The facts have to be recognised, but there can be a too easy learning, backed by solid information and careful argument, of such hopelessness and such frustrations. These can pass for humane wisdom, or for critical intelligence. William Cobbett is then only this quirky individual, this attractive old roaring man. None of his kind or succession matters, until time and distance set in, and the dignity and courage can be suitably framed by the intervening failures: the repeated hopelessness, the recurrent frustrations. Most current observers and commentators, including that large corps of retrospective radicals — a piquant and colourful liberalism within a conforming *rentier* culture — know that the only good radical is a dead, failed one. Recognitions of cause and courage come ready wrapped in distance, defeat, and those intimations of irrelevance which ratify resignation and non-involvement. Quirky lost men and causes, all.

Such confident despair! So subtle and energetic a sapping of wills! So insinuating a motion that this disturbing presence 'should be *put out of the room*!'.

In fact he keeps getting up: 'that they might see the man'. He does not ask permission or approval, least of all from the privileged or the worldly-wise. There is a challenge, and it has to be made. There is an argument, and it has to be carried on.

Further reading

Much of Cobbett's most interesting writing first appeared in his *Political Register*, which was published (with some variations of title and one break) from 1802 to 1835 and is available in collected form in some specialist libraries in Volumes I to LXXXVIII. Extracts from the *Register* have appeared in several publications. *Cobbett's Two-Penny Trash* was issued monthly, with one break, from July 1830 to July 1832, and printed in two volumes in 1831–2. *Eleven Lectures on the French and Belgian Revolutions and English Boroughmongering*, given from August to October 1830 in London, were printed in 1830.

Books by Cobbett available in modern editions

Life and Adventures of Peter Porcupine (1796); ed. G. D. H. Cole, 1927; reprinted Kennikat Press, 1970.

A Grammar of the English Language, in a series of letters (1818); ed. H. L. Stephen, 1906.

Cottage Economy (1822). Oxford University Press paperback, 1979.

The English Gardener (1829). Oxford University Press paperback, 1979.

Rural Rides (1830); ed. G. D. H. and M. Cole, 3 vols, 1930. See also Everyman and Penguin editions.

Advice to Young Men (1830). Oxford University Press paperback, 1980.

Collections and selections

Porcupine's Works, 12 vols, 1801.

William Cobbett: Selections, ed. A. M. D. Hughes, 1923.

The Opinions of William Cobbett, ed. G. D. H. and M. Cole, 1944.

Some books about Cobbett

The Life of William Cobbett, by G. D. H. Cole. Revised edition, 1947. Still the best general introduction to Cobbett.

William Cobbett: The Poor Man's Friend, by G. Spater, 2 vols, Cambridge University Press, 1982. A modern biography, with some new information.

The Life and Letters of William Cobbett, by L. Melville, 2 vols, 1913. Still of interest.

William Cobbett, by John W. Osborne, Rutgers University Press, 1966. A systematic analysis of some of Cobbett's ideas.

Peter Porcupine in America, by M. E. Clark, 1939. A detailed study of Cobbett's involvements in American politics in the 1790s.

William Cobbett, by James Sambrook, Routledge and Kegan Paul, 1973. An alternative reading of Cobbett.

Bibliographies

William Cobbett: A Bibliographical Account of His Life and Times, by M. L. Pearl, 1953.

William Cobbett and the United States 1792–1835: A Bibliography with Notes and Extracts, by P. W. Gaines, 1971.

Index